SOUNDS and LETTERS

FOR

Readers and Spellers

**Phonemic Awareness Drills for
Teachers and Speech-Language Pathologists**

Jane Fell Greene, Ed.D.

04   03   02   01   00   10   9   8   7   6

ISBN 1-57035-126-0

Edited by Raven Moore
Text layout and design by Kimberly Harris
Cover design by Tracy Katzenberger
Production assistance by Denise Geddis
Illustrations by Andrea Hergenreder

Printed in the United States of America

Published and Distributed by

Sopris West

Helping You Meet the Needs of At-Risk Students

4093 Specialty Place • Longmont, CO 80504 • (303) 651-2829
www.sopriswest.com

Acknowledgments

Sounds and Letters is dedicated to my friend and colleague, Louisa Moats. Her work will make literacy a reality for millions of children.

—Jane Fell Greene, Ed.D., June, 2000

Table of Contents

Introduction

Phonemic awareness is the innate knowledge that (1) Discrete speech sounds (phonemes) constitute words, and (2) Manipulating speech sounds can create new words. Science documents that phonemic awareness is the most potent predictor of success in learning to read. Phonemic awareness is more highly related to reading than are tests of general intelligence, reading readiness, and listening comprehension. Conversely, lack of phonemic awareness is the most powerful determinant of the likelihood of failure to learn to read, because of the importance of phonemic awareness in learning the English alphabetic system (Moats, 1997).

For students with delays in reading and/or spelling, phonemic awareness has repeatedly been documented as a core deficit. But phonemic awareness *can be taught* to students who do not naturally possess it. Students can develop phonemic awareness and can become good readers and spellers.

Phonemic awareness comprises a hierarchy of cognitive abilities. In *Sounds and Letters*, this hierarchy is reflected in increasingly difficult tasks, through the eight stages of phonemic awareness development. These stages are:

1. Phoneme production/replication
2. Phoneme isolation
3. Phoneme segmentation and counting
4. Phoneme blending
5. Rhyming
6. Phoneme deletion
7. Phoneme substitution
8. Phoneme reversal

A ninth activity, Pig Latin, is also included for each unit. Although it is not a formally designated stage of phonemic awareness, Pig Latin is an excellent way to increase phonemic awareness and is fun for students.

The Phonology Concepts section at the beginning of each unit lists the new and review concepts included in that unit. The drills, designed for classroom or clinic, are administered orally. Simply select a few drills, or parts of drills, with which to introduce each lesson. A single unit may constitute parts of several days' lesson plans. The 18 units are carefully designed to be taught in sequential order; each unit's contents are dependent upon previously mastered content.

Once students have mastered a unit's new phonology concepts, begin teaching students to associate phonemes with graphemes (sounds with letters). A Reading/Spelling Vocabulary list is provided for each unit; this list contains many of the words which can be built using the phoneme/grapheme correspondences presented up to and including that unit. For some units, nonphonetic vocabulary words are included also; these appear in italic type. (The *Sounds and Letters Cards*, also available from Sopris West, provide the basis for developing students' reading/spelling vocabularies using a variety of activities.)

Phonemic awareness provides the critical "jump start" to reading and spelling, but it is not the entirety of reading or spelling. Reading, writing, and spelling all require complex, simultaneous cognitive and linguistic processing. This book may be used as a standalone product, but it is also a component of the comprehensive *LANGUAGE !* curriculum, which is based in current research and designed especially for students with delays in the acquisition of reading, writing, and spelling. *LANGUAGE !* is far more than a reading program. Although the code of written language constitutes a core strand through its curriculum, *LANGUAGE !* is comprised of fifteen integrated language arts strands. (For more information about the curriculum, refer to the end of this book.)

This 18-unit series of phonemic awareness drills is based in current science. Whether these drills are used with young children, adults, or middle schoolers who are delayed in reading or spelling acquisition, they will help to develop the phonemic awareness that provides the critical foundation, the firm base required for mastery of reading and spelling.

Multisensory Techniques for Phonemic Awareness Drills

Multisensory teaching can produce a dramatic increase in retention of information. Following is a set of hand and arm movements developed for use with this book's phonemic awareness tasks; these techniques will provide the important multisensory component when you conduct these drills with your students.

Practice these techniques and become familiar with them in advance before you use them with your students. Remember, phonemic awareness activities should precede phoneme-grapheme correspondence activities. Also, keep in mind that no letter images are used during phonemic awareness drills.

Anchor the Word

Most of the following techniques will begin with this arm motion, which will help to "anchor" the word or phoneme in the students' memories: Hold your left arm out to the side, elbow bent, hand in a fist with the palm side facing the students. As you say the target word or phoneme, move your bent elbow down a few inches. Have the students make the same motion with their right arms as they join you in saying the word or phoneme. Say the word or phoneme two times.

Stage 1: Phoneme Replication

Repeat the Sounds (Auditory Reinforcement): Begin with your left arm and the students' right arms in position as for the anchor motion (as described previously). Say the target phoneme twice and have the students repeat it each time (you should repeat the phoneme along with them). As the phoneme is spoken, both you and the students should move your bent elbows down a few inches. Example: "Say */m/.*" (Response: "*/m/.*") "Say */m/.*" (Response: "*/m/.*")

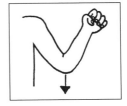

Stage 2: Phoneme Isolation

Anchor the Word: Anchor the word two times. Example: "Say **mat**." (Response: "**mat**.") "Say **mat**." (Response: "**mat**.")

Isolate a Phoneme: Example: "Say the first sound in **mat**." (Response: "*/m/.*")

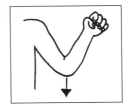

Stage 3: Phoneme Segmentation

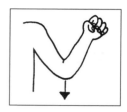

Anchor the Word: Anchor the word two times.

Segment the Sounds: Place your left arm and the students' right arms in position as for the anchor motion. Beginning with the thumb, raise one finger at a time in association with each phoneme in a word. Example:

1. Direct the students: "Say the sounds of **stop**."

2. Raise the thumb while saying /s/.

3. Raise the index finger while saying /t/.

4. Raise the middle finger while saying /o/.

5. Raise the ring finger while saying /p/.

6. Have the students make a fist again and move their fists left to right at shoulder level while saying **stop**. Simultaneously, you move your fist right to left while saying **stop**.

Remember, each finger is raised while saying each separate phoneme.

Stage 4: Phoneme Blending

This is the only stage during which you do not begin by saying the target word twice. (In this stage, the word is the answer).

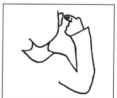 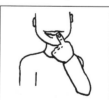

Initiate the visual-auditory-tactile-kinesthetic technique by saying "Listen" (place your index finger at your ear) "and repeat" (place your index finger at your mouth); "listen and repeat." Then you model and the students repeat the word's phonemes three times.

Each time you repeat, your fingers come closer together. Lastly, you and the students blend the sounds together to form the word, moving your fists horizontally. The students use their right arms, palms outward (facing you), moving left to right. You use your left arm, palm outward (facing the students), moving right to left, mirroring the students. Example:

1. Raise the thumb while saying /s/.

2. Raise the index finger while saying /t/.

3. Raise the middle finger while saying /o/.

4. Raise the ring finger while saying /p/.

5. Say the individual phonemes again in quicker succession, moving the raised fingers closer together.

6. Say the individual phonemes again in even quicker succession, closing up the space between the raised fingers.

1st time   2nd time   3rd time

7. Have the students make a fist with their right hands and move their fists left to right at shoulder level while saying **stop**; simultaneously you move your fist right to left while saying **stop**.

Stage 5: Rhyming

Anchor the Word

Create a Rhyme: Say the target word twice and have the students repeat it each time. Then simply request a rhyming word, and do the anchor motion when the students respond. Example: "Say a word that rhymes with **mat**."

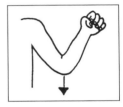

Stage 6: Phoneme Deletion

Anchor the Word

Delete a Phoneme: Say the target word twice and have the students repeat it each time. Ask the students to delete a phoneme from a word, and do the anchor motion when the students respond. Example: "Say **mat** without the /m/."

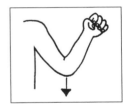

Stage 7: Phoneme Substitution

Anchor the Word

Substitute a Phoneme: Ask the students to delete and substitute a phoneme within a word, and do the anchor motion when the students respond. Example: "Say **mat**. Now change the first sound to /s/." (Response: "**sat**.")

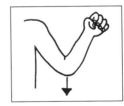

Stage 8: Phoneme Reversal

Phoneme reversal is the most cognitively and linguistically challenging phonemic awareness task. This task requires much modeling and practice, and is a critical phoneme manipulation task. Note that the arms are different for this stage than for the other stages: The students will begin with their left arms and you will begin with your right arm. Use the following technique for phoneme reversal:

1. Anchor the word (with right arm). When anchoring the word with your right arm, your arm should be slightly in front of your body, rather than directly to the side, to allow for the next movements.

2. Say: "Now, change the first sound to last . . ." (while saying this, move your right forearm down to a horizontal position) ". . . and the last sound to first." (While saying this, move your left forearm down, ending with your left forearm horizontal atop your right forearm.)

3. Provide adequate wait time for students to process the task before extending both arms horizontally forward, elbows bent, palms up (as if "catching" the word) as the students provide the answer. Example:

   a. Direct the students: "Say **pal**." (Students respond: "**pal**.") Do this twice.

   b. Students and teacher together: "Now, change the first sound to last . . . (the students move their left elbows forward and left forearms down to a horizontal position) ". . . and the last sound to first." (The students move their right elbows forward and right forearms down, ending with their right forearms horizontal atop their left forearms.)

   c. As the students say the answer, you and they should simultaneously extend both forearms horizontally forward, arms bent at the elbow, palms up.

Stage 9: Pig Latin

Pig Latin is an extra "for fun" exercise to increase phonemic awareness. Use the Anchor the Word technique to ensure that the students have heard the target word before proceeding with each Pig Latin activity.

Unit Directory

Unit 1: A phoneme is a single unit of sound. A grapheme is a symbol, a letter.

    A. Consonant phonemes are closed sounds.

    B. Vowel phonemes are open sounds.

    C. Every word has a vowel phoneme.

    Sound-letter (phoneme-grapheme) relationships: short /*a*/, **t**, **s**, **m**, **b**, **c**, **f**

Unit 2: Sound-letter relationships: **r**, **h**, **j**, **n**, **l**, **p**

Unit 3: Sound-letter relationships: hard **g**, **d**, **v**

Unit 4: Vowel phoneme concept: Every word has a vowel sound (phoneme).

    Sound-letter relationships: short /*i*/, **w**

Unit 5: Sound-letter relationships: **k**, **ck**

Unit 6: Place value for encoding: **-ck**

Unit 7: Sound-letter relationships: **qu**, **x**, **y**, **z**

Unit 8: Vowel phoneme concept: Every word has a vowel sound (phoneme).

    Sound-letter relationship: short /*o*/

Unit 9: Place value for encoding doubled consonant letters (graphemes): **-ss**, **-ll**, **-ff**, **-zz**

Unit 10: Sound-letter relationships: **-ng**, **-nk**

Unit 11: Consonant digraphs are two consonant letters (graphemes) that represent one consonant sound (phoneme): **wh**, **th**, **sh**, **ch**.

Unit 12: Vowel phoneme concept: Every word has a vowel sound (phoneme).

    Sound-letter relationship: short /*e*/

Unit 13: Initial blends are consonant pairs representing two different consonant sounds (phonemes) at the beginning of a word: **bl-**, **gl-**, **cl-**, **pl-**, **fl-**, **sl-**, **bl-**, **fr-**, **tr-**, **cr-**, **dr-**, **gr-**, **pr-**, **shr-**, **thr-**, **sc-**, **sm-**, **sn-**, **sp-**, **sk-**, **st-**, **squ-**, **sw-**, **tw-**, **dw-**.

Unit 14: Vowel phoneme concept: Every word has a vowel sound (phoneme).

Sound-letter relationship: short /u/

Unit 15: Phoneme/syllable analysis: phoneme-syllable-word relationships:

A. A word must have at least one vowel sound (phoneme).

B. A word has one or more syllables.

C. Each syllable contains one vowel sound (phoneme).

Unit 16: Clusters are three consonant letters representing three different consonant sounds (phonemes): **st-**, **spr-**, **spl-**, **scr-**.

Unit 17: Final blends are consonant letter pairs representing two different consonant sounds (phonemes) at the end of a word: **-st**, **-sk**, **-sp**, **-nt**, **-nd**, **-mp**, **-ld**, **-lk**, **-lp**, **-lt**, **-ft**, **-pt**, **-ct**.

Unit 18: The phoneme /ch/ is encoded **-tch** after short vowels at the ends of one-syllable words:

Examples: **crutch, latch, notch, pitch, hatch, witch**

Exceptions: **such, rich, much, which**

Advancing to Levels 2 and 3 of *LANGUAGE !*

Upon completion of Unit 18 of the *LANGUAGE !* curriculum, all five short vowels; closed syllables; initial and final consonant blends; and consonant clusters have been mastered, along with several spelling rules. With a solid foundation of phonemic awareness skills in place, the students should then be ready to move on to Levels 2 and 3 of the *LANGUAGE !* curriculum. Beginning with Unit 19, syllable types and their inherent vowel differences (**r**-control, open syllables, final silent **-e**, vowel digraphs, diphthongs, and final stable syllable **c** + **-le**) are sequentially and cumulatively mastered. In Levels 2 and 3, morphemes from Anglo-Saxon, Latin, and Greek are introduced. The grammar of English is taught sequentially and cumulatively and is integrated and woven through a structured composition strand. The curriculum continues to emphasize comprehension of narrative and expository text, through all of the levels of Bloom's *Taxonomy*. Contextual analysis and critical reading are emphasized at levels 2 and 3. All fifteen language arts strands develop in Levels 2 and 3, but Level 3 provides for mastery of more advanced principles of grammar, composition, and literature.

Unit 1

Phonemic Awareness Drills

These sequential, cumulative drills assess and build phonemic awareness in emerging readers and spellers. To initiate daily lessons, present portions of these drills orally—without corresponding letters. Phonemes (sounds) should be mastered before they are associated with their orthographic representations (letters). After phonemic awareness has been established for a unit's new phonology concepts, students can be introduced to the unit's new symbol-sound correspondences and its reading/spelling vocabulary.

Phonology Concepts for Unit 1

A phoneme is a sound. A grapheme is a letter.

- Consonant phonemes are closed sounds: /t/, /s/, /m/, /b/, /k/, /f/.

- Vowel phonemes are open sounds: short /a/.

- Every word has a vowel sound (phoneme).

- Sound-letter (phoneme-grapheme) relationships: **<u>a</u>** (short /a/), **<u>t</u>**, **<u>s</u>**, **<u>m</u>**, **<u>b</u>**, **<u>c</u>**, **<u>f</u>**

Stage 1: Phoneme Production/Replication

(Teacher Note: Example words containing the isolated phonemes for this unit are provided. Some students may not need these examples, and may produce the phonemes based on your modeling alone. Example words are provided for students who need them, however.)

Have the students: 1) repeat each isolated phoneme; and 2) try to describe differences between phoneme pairs:

Repeat these sounds:

/a/	/t/	/s/	/m/	/b/	/k/	/f/
am	tan	sat	mat	bat	cat	fat

Stage 2: Phoneme Isolation

Say **am**. (Repeat **am**.) Say **am**. (Repeat **am**.) What's the first sound in **am**?   (/a/) (short **<u>a</u>**)

Say **am**. (Repeat **am**.) Say **am**. (Repeat **am**.) What's the last sound in **am**?   (/m/)

Say **bat**. (Repeat **bat**.) Say **bat**. (Repeat **bat**.) What's the first sound in **bat**?   (/b/)

Say **fat**. (Repeat **fat**.) Say **fat**. (Repeat **fat**.) What's the first sound in **fat**?   (/f/)

Say **fat**. (Repeat **fat**.) Say **fat**. (Repeat **fat**.) What's the last sound in **fat**?   (/t/)

Say **cab**. (Repeat **cab**.) Say **cab**. (Repeat **cab**.) What's the middle sound in **cab**?   (/a/) (short **a**)

Say **cat**. (Repeat **cat**.) Say **cat**. (Repeat **cat**.) What's the first sound in **cat**?   (/k/)

Say **mat**. (Repeat **mat**.) Say **mat**. (Repeat **mat**.) What's the last sound in **mat**?   (/t/)

Say **mat**. (Repeat **mat**.) Say **mat**. (Repeat **mat**.) What's the middle sound in **mat**?   (/a/) (short **a**)

Say **mat**. (Repeat **mat**.) Say **mat**. (Repeat **mat**.) What's the first sound in **mat**?   (/m/)

Say **Sam**. (Repeat **Sam**.) Say **Sam**. (Repeat **Sam**.)
What's the middle sound in **Sam**?   (/a/) (short **a**)

Say **tam**. (Repeat **tam**.) Say **tam**. (Repeat **tam**.) What's the last sound in **tam**?   (/m/)

Say **back**. (Repeat **back**.) Say **back**. (Repeat **back**.)
What's the first sound in **back**?   (/b/)

Stage 3: Phoneme Segmentation and Counting (Spelling the Sounds)

Say **mat**. (Repeat **mat**.) Say **mat**. (Repeat **mat**.) Say the sounds in **mat**.   (/m/ /a/ /t/)

Say **sat**. (Repeat **sat**.) Say **sat**. (Repeat **sat**.) Say the sounds in **sat**.   (/s/ /a/ /t/)

Say **cab**. (Repeat **cab**.) Say **cab**. (Repeat **cab**.) Say the sounds in **cab**.   (/k/ /a/ /b/)

Say **am**. (Repeat **am**.) Say **am**. (Repeat **am**.) Say the sounds in **am**.   (/a/ /m/)

Say **cat**. (Repeat **cat**.) Say **cat**. (Repeat **cat**.) Say the sounds in **cat**.   (/k/ /a/ /t/)

Say **at**. (Repeat **at**.) Say **at**. (Repeat **at**.) Say the sounds in **at**.   (/a/ /t/)

Say **fat**. (Repeat **fat**.) Say **fat**. (Repeat **fat**.) Say the sounds in **fat**.   (/f/ /a/ /t/)

Say **tam**. (Repeat **tam**.) Say **tam**. (Repeat **tam**.) Say the sounds in **tam**.   (/t/ /a/ /m/)

Say **bat**. (Repeat **bat**.) Say **bat**. (Repeat **bat**.) Say the sounds in **bat**.   (/b/ /a/ /t/)

Say **bam**. (Repeat **bam**.) Say **bam**. (Repeat **bam**.) Say the sounds in **bam**.   (/b/ /a/ /m/)

After the students have been introduced to the new unit's vocabulary words, you may ask, "How many sounds in **xxx**?" How many letters in **xxx**?"

Stage 4: Phoneme Blending

Listen and repeat. Listen and repeat: /a/ /m/. (Repeat phoneme series three times.)   (am)

Listen and repeat. Listen and repeat: /b/ /a/ /m/. (Repeat phoneme series three times.)   (bam)

Listen and repeat. Listen and repeat: /t/ /a/ /m/. (Repeat phoneme series three times.)   (tam)

Listen and repeat. Listen and repeat: /s/ /a/ /m/. (Repeat phoneme series three times.)   (Sam)

Listen and repeat. Listen and repeat: /s/ /a/ /t/. (Repeat phoneme series three times.)   (sat)

Listen and repeat. Listen and repeat: /m/ /a/ /t/. (Repeat phoneme series three times.)   (mat)

Listen and repeat. Listen and repeat: /b/ /a/ /t/. (Repeat phoneme series three times.)   (bat)

Stage 5: Rhyming

Say **sat**. (Repeat **sat**.) Say **sat**. (Repeat **sat**.)
Say a word that rhymes with **sat**.   (hat, bat, cat, at)

Say **cab**. (Repeat **cab**.) Say **cab**. (Repeat **cab**.)
Say a word that rhymes with **cab**.   (tab, nab, lab, stab)

Say **tam**. (Repeat **tam**.) Say **tam**. (Repeat **tam**.)
Say a word that rhymes with **tam**.   (ham, Sam, lamb, bam)

Say **cat**. (Repeat **cat**.) Say **cat**. (Repeat **cat**.)
Say a word that rhymes with **cat**.   (hat, bat, sat, at)

Say **bam**. (Repeat **bam**.) Say **bam**. (Repeat **bam**.)
Say a word that rhymes with **bam**.   (ham, Sam, lamb, am)

Say **am**. (Repeat **am**.) Say **am**. (Repeat **am**.)
Say a word that rhymes with **am**.   (ham, Sam, lamb, bam)

Say **at**. (Repeat **at**.) Say **at**. (Repeat **at**.)
Say a word that rhymes with **at**.   (hat, bat, cat, pat)

Say **bat**. (Repeat **bat**.) Say **bat**. (Repeat **bat**.)
Say a word that rhymes with **bat**.   (hat, slat, cat, mat)

Stage 6: Phoneme Deletion

Say **at**. (Repeat **at**.) Say **at**. (Repeat **at**.) Say **at** without the /t/.   (/a/)

Say **cab**. (Repeat **cab**.) Say **cab**. (Repeat **cab**.) Say **cab** without the /k/.   (/ab/)

Say **bam**. (Repeat **bam**.) Say **bam**. (Repeat **bam**.) Say **bam** without the /b/.   (/am/)

Say **tab**. (Repeat **tab**.) Say **tab**. (Repeat **tab**.) Say **tab** without the /b/.   (/ta/)

Say **bat**. (Repeat **bat**.) Say **bat**. (Repeat **bat**.) Say **bat** without the /b/.   (/at/)

Say **cat**. (Repeat **cat**.) Say **cat**. (Repeat **cat**.) Say **cat** without the /t/.   (/ka/)

Say **mat**. (Repeat **mat**.) Say **mat**. (Repeat **mat**.) Say **mat** without the /m/.   (at)

Say **Sam**. (Repeat **Sam**.) Say **Sam**. (Repeat **Sam**.) Say **Sam** without the /s/.   (/am/)

Stage 7: Phoneme Substitution

Say **sat**. (Repeat **sat**.) Say **sat**. (Repeat **sat**.) Now, change the first sound in **sat** to /k/.   (cat)

Say **mat**. (Repeat **mat**.) Say **mat**. (Repeat **mat**.) Now, change the first sound in **mat** to /t/.   (tat)

Say **cab**. (Repeat **cab**.) Say **cab**. (Repeat **cab**.) Now, change the first sound in **cab** to /t/.   (tab)

Say **bat**. (Repeat **bat**.) Say **bat**. (Repeat **bat**.) Now, change the first sound in **bat** to /s/.   (sat)

Say **map**. (Repeat **map**.) Say **map**. (Repeat **map**.) Now, change the first sound in **map** to /k/. (cap)

Say **bat**. (Repeat **bat**.) Say **bat**. (Repeat **bat**.) Now, change the first sound in **bat** to /f/.   (fat)

Advancement: After initial phoneme(s), substitute final phoneme(s):

Say **cab**. (Repeat **cab**.) Say **cab**. (Repeat **cab**.) Now, change the last sound in **cab** to /t/.   (cat)

Say **bam**. (Repeat **bam**.) Say **bam**. (Repeat **bam**.) Now, change the last sound in **bam** to /t/.   (bat)

Say **cam**. (Repeat **cam**.) Say **cam**. (Repeat **cam**.) Now, change the last sound in **cam** to /b/. (cab)

Say **fab**. (Repeat **fab**.) Say **fab**. (Repeat **fab**.) Now, change the last sound in **fab** to /t/.   (fat)

Say **bat**. (Repeat **bat**.) Say **bat**. (Repeat **bat**.) Now, change the last sound in **bat** to /m/.   (bam)

Say **tab**. (Repeat **tab**.) Say **tab**. (Repeat **tab**.) Now, change the last sound in **tab** to /m/.   (tam)

Say **back**. (Repeat **back**.) Say **back**. (Repeat **back**.) Now, change the last sound in **back** to /t/. (bat)

Stage 8: Phoneme Reversal

Say **mat**. (Repeat **mat**.) Say **mat**. (Repeat **mat**.)
Now, change the first sound to last, and the last sound to first.   (tam)

Say **back**. (Repeat **back**.) Say **back**. (Repeat **back**.)
Now, change the first sound to last, and the last sound to first.   (cab)

Say **tab**. (Repeat **tab**.) Say **tab**. (Repeat **tab**.)
Now, change the first sound to last, and the last sound to first.   (bat)

Say **Mac**. (Repeat **Mac**.) Say **Mac**. (Repeat **Mac**.)
Now, change the first sound to last, and the last sound to first.   (cam)

Say **tam**. (Repeat **tam**.) Say **tam**. (Repeat **tam**.)
Now, change the first sound to last, and the last sound to first.   (mat)

Say **bat**. (Repeat **bat**.) Say **bat**. (Repeat **bat**.)
Now, change the first sound to last, and the last sound to first.   (tab)

Stage 9: Pig Latin

Three or four modelings may be necessary with this activity, particularly for students with a significant lack of phonemic awareness. Do not penalize students who cannot master Pig Latin.

Say **bat**. (Repeat **bat**.) Say **bat**. (Repeat **bat**.) Say **bat** without the /b/.	(/at/)
Say /at/. (Repeat /at/.) Say /at/. (Repeat /at/.) Say /at/ with /b/ at the end.	(/at b/)
Now, say /ay/ at the end.	(/at bay/)
Say **cab**. (Repeat **cab**.) Say **cab**. (Repeat **cab**.) Say **cab** without the /k/.	(/ab/)
Say /ab/. (Repeat /ab/.) Say /ab/. (Repeat /ab/.) Say /ab/ with /k/ at the end.	(/ab k/)
Now, say /ay/ at the end.	(/ab kay/)
Say **sat**. (Repeat **sat**.) Say **sat**. (Repeat **sat**.) Say **sat** without the /s/.	(/at/)
Say /at/. (Repeat /at/.) Say /at/. (Repeat /at/.) Say /at/ with /s/ at the end.	(/at s/)
Now, say /ay/ at the end.	(/at say/)
Say **tab**. (Repeat **tab**.) Say **tab**. (Repeat **tab**.) Say **tab** without the /t/.	(/ab/)
Say /ab/. (Repeat /ab/.) Say /ab/. (Repeat /ab/.) Say /ab/ with /t/ at the end.	(/ab t/)
Now, say /ay/ at the end.	(/ab tay/)
Say **fat**. (Repeat **fat**.) Say **fat**. (Repeat **fat**.) Say **fat** without the /f/.	(/at/)
Say /at/. (Repeat /at/.) Say /at/. (Repeat /at/.) Say /at/ with /f/ at the end.	(/at f/)
Now, say /ay/ at the end.	(/at fay/)
Now, say together in Pig Latin: "I can speak Pig Latin."	(Iay ancay eakspay igpay atinlay)

Suggestions for Related Activities

- Introduce some morphologic awareness activities using familiar compound words:
  - Say **cowboy** without the **cow**. (boy)
  - Say **sunset** without the **sun**. (set)

- Introduce some syntactic awareness activities:
Say "The dog ran." Now, change the sentence to a question.   (Did the dog run?)

Reading/Spelling Vocabulary

at	cab	mat	Tab
bam	cat	Sam	Tam
bat	fat	sat	*a*

Unit 2

Phonemic Awareness Drills

These sequential, cumulative drills assess and build phonemic awareness in emerging readers and spellers. To initiate daily lessons, present portions of these drills orally—without corresponding letters. Phonemes (sounds) should be mastered before they are associated with their orthographic representations (letters). After phonemic awareness has been established for a unit's new phonology concepts, students can be introduced to the unit's new symbol-sound correspondences and its reading/spelling vocabulary.

Phonology Concepts for Unit 2

A phoneme is a sound. A grapheme is a letter.

- Consonant phonemes are closed sounds:

    - Review: /t/, /s/, /m/, /b/, /k/, /f/

    - New: /r/, /h/, /j/, /n/, /l/, /p/

- Vowel phonemes are open sounds. Review: short /a/

- Every word has a vowel phoneme.

- Sound-letter (phoneme-grapheme) relationships:

    - Review: **t**, **s**, **m**, **b**, **c**, **f**

    - New: **r**, **h**, **j**, **n**, **l**, **p**

Stage 1: Phoneme Production/Replication

Have the students repeat each isolated phoneme:

- Repeat these sounds:

/a/	/t/	/s/	/m/	/b/	/k/	/f/
am	tan	sat	mat	bat	cat	fat

- Repeat these new sounds:

/r/	/h/	/j/	/n/	/l/	/p/
ran	hat	jab	nab	lap	pat

Stage 2: Phoneme Isolation

Say **an.** (Repeat **an.**) Say **an.** (Repeat **an.**) What's the first sound in **an**?	*(/a/) (short **a**)*
Say **an.** (Repeat **an.**) Say **an.** (Repeat **an.**) What's the last sound in **an**?	*(/n/)*
Say **ban.** (Repeat **ban.**) Say **ban.** (Repeat **ban.**) What's the first sound in **ban**?	*(/b/)*
Say **fan.** (Repeat **fan.**) Say **fan.** (Repeat **fan.**) What's the first sound in **fan**?	*(/f/)*
Say **pal.** (Repeat **pal.**) Say **pal.** (Repeat **pal.**) What's the last sound in **pal**?	*(/l/)*
Say **rap.** (Repeat **rap.**) Say **rap.** (Repeat **rap.**) What's the middle sound in **rap**?	*(/a/) (short **a**)*
Say **rap.** (Repeat **rap.**) Say **rap.** (Repeat **rap.**) What's the first sound in **rap**?	*(/r/)*
Say **rap.** (Repeat **rap.**) Say **rap.** (Repeat **rap.**) What's the last sound in **rap**?	*(/p/)*
Say **lap.** (Repeat **lap.**) Say **lap.** (Repeat **lap.**) What's the middle sound in **lap**?	*(/a/) (short **a**)*
Say **lap.** (Repeat **lap.**) Say **lap.** (Repeat **lap.**) What's the first sound in **lap**?	*(/l/)*
Say **Sam.** (Repeat **Sam.**) Say **Sam.** (Repeat **Sam.**) What's the middle sound in **Sam**?	*(/a/) (short **a**)*
Say **jam.** (Repeat **jam.**) Say **jam.** (Repeat **jam.**) What's the last sound in **jam**?	*(/m/)*
Say **jam.** (Repeat **jam.**) Say **jam.** (Repeat **jam.**) What's the first sound in **jam**?	*(/j/)*
Say **ram.** (Repeat **ram.**) Say **ram.** (Repeat **ram.**) What's the first sound in **ram**?	*(/r/)*
Say **ham.** (Repeat **ham.**) Say **ham.** (Repeat **ham.**) What's the last sound in **ham**?	*(/m/)*
Say **pat.** (Repeat **pat.**) Say **pat.** (Repeat **pat.**) What's the first sound in **pat**?	*(/p/)*
Say **hat.** (Repeat **hat.**) Say **hat.** (Repeat **hat.**) What's the last sound in **hat**?	*(/t/)*
Say **jab.** (Repeat **jab.**) Say **jab.** (Repeat **jab.**) What's the last sound in **jab**?	*(/b/)*

Stage 3: Phoneme Segmentation and Counting (Spelling the Sounds)

Say **jab.** (Repeat **jab.**) Say **jab.** (Repeat **jab.**) Say the sounds in **jab**.	*(/j/ /a/ /b/)*
Say **pan.** (Repeat **pan.**) Say **pan.** (Repeat **pan.**) Say the sounds in **pan**.	*(/p/ /a/ /n/)*
Say **hat.** (Repeat **hat.**) Say **hat.** (Repeat **hat.**) Say the sounds in **hat**.	*(/h/ /a/ /t/)*
Say **am.** (Repeat **am.**) Say **am.** (Repeat **am.**) Say the sounds in **am**.	*(/a/ /m/)*
Say **jam.** (Repeat **jam.**) Say **jam.** (Repeat **jam.**) Say the sounds in **jam**.	*(/j/ /a/ /m/)*
Say **nab.** (Repeat **nab.**) Say **nab.** (Repeat **nab.**) Say the sounds in **nab**.	*(/n/ /a/ /b/)*
Say **fan.** (Repeat **fan.**) Say **fan.** (Repeat **fan.**) Say the sounds in **fan**.	*(/f/ /a/ /n/)*
Say **at.** (Repeat **at.**) Say **at.** (Repeat **at.**) Say the sounds in **at**.	*(/a/ /t/)*

Say **can**. (Repeat **can**.) Say **can**. (Repeat **can**.) Say the sounds in **can**. *(/c/ /a/ /n/)*

Say **ram**. (Repeat **ram**.) Say **ram**. (Repeat **ram**.) Say the sounds in **ram**. *(/r/ /a/ /m/)*

Say **rat**. (Repeat **rat**.) Say **rat**. (Repeat **rat**.) Say the sounds in **rat**. *(/r/ /a/ /t/)*

Say **an**. (Repeat **an**.) Say **an**. (Repeat **an**.) Say the sounds in **an**. *(/a/ /n/)*

After the students have been introduced to the new unit's vocabulary words, you may ask, "How many sounds in **xxx**?" "How many letters in **xxx**?"

Stage 4: Phoneme Blending

Listen and repeat. Listen and repeat: /a/ /n/. (Repeat phoneme series three times.) (an)

Listen and repeat. Listen and repeat: /b/ /a/ /n/. (Repeat phoneme series three times.) (ban)

Listen and repeat. Listen and repeat: /t/ /a/ /n/. (Repeat phoneme series three times.) (tan)

Listen and repeat. Listen and repeat: /h/ /a/ /m/. (Repeat phoneme series three times.) (ham)

Listen and repeat. Listen and repeat: /j/ /a/ /m/. (Repeat phoneme series three times.) (jam)

Listen and repeat. Listen and repeat: /n/ /a/ /b/. (Repeat phoneme series three times.) (nab)

Listen and repeat. Listen and repeat: /r/ /a/ /t/. (Repeat phoneme series three times.) (rat)

Listen and repeat. Listen and repeat: /r/ /a/ /n/. (Repeat phoneme series three times.) (ran)

Listen and repeat. Listen and repeat: /r/ /a/ /m/. (Repeat phoneme series three times.) (ram)

Stage 5: Rhyming

Say **ran**. (Repeat **ran**.) Say **ran**. (Repeat **ran**.)
Say a word that rhymes with **ran**. (man, ban, can, fan)

Say **jam**. (Repeat **jam**.) Say **jam**. (Repeat **jam**.)
Say a word that rhymes with **jam**. (ham, bam, cam, Sam)

Say **hat**. (Repeat **hat**.) Say **hat**. (Repeat **hat**.)
Say a word that rhymes with **hat**. (bat, cat, fat, mat)

Say **nab**. (Repeat **nab**.) Say **nab**. (Repeat **nab**.)
Say a word that rhymes with **nab**. (cab, gab, jab, lab)

Say **pan**. (Repeat **pan**.) Say **pan**. (Repeat **pan**.)
Say a word that rhymes with **pan**. (ran, can, Dan, fan)

Say **sap**. (Repeat **sap**.) Say **sap**. (Repeat **sap**.)
Say a word that rhymes with **sap**. (tap, lap, rap, map)

Say **rap**. (Repeat **rap**.) Say **rap**. (Repeat **rap**.)
Say a word that rhymes with **rap**.　　　　　　　　　　　　　(map, nap, cap, lap)

Say **pal**. (Repeat **pal**.) Say **pal**. (Repeat **pal**.)
Say a word that rhymes with **pal**.　　　　　　　　　　　　　(Al, gal, Hal, Sal)

Stage 6: Phoneme Deletion

Say **jam**. (Repeat **jam**.) Say **jam**. (Repeat **jam**.) Say **jam** without the /j/.　　　*(/am/)*

Say **can**. (Repeat **can**.) Say **can**. (Repeat **can**.) Say **can** without the /k/.　　　*(/an/)*

Say **rat**. (Repeat **rat**.) Say **rat**. (Repeat **rat**.) Say **rat** without the /r/.　　　*(/at/)*

Say **lab**. (Repeat **lab**.) Say **lab**. (Repeat **lab**.) Say **lab** without the /l/.　　　*(/ab/)*

Say **hat**. (Repeat **hat**.) Say **hat**. (Repeat **hat**.) Say **hat** without the /h/.　　　*(/at/)*

Say **hat**. (Repeat **hat**.) Say **hat**. (Repeat **hat**.) Say **hat** without the /t/.　　　*(/ha/)*

Say **man**. (Repeat **man**.) Say **man**. (Repeat **man**.) Say **man** without the /m/.　　　*(/an/)*

Say **pan**. (Repeat **pan**.) Say **pan**. (Repeat **pan**.) Say **pan** without the /p/.　　　*(/an/)*

Say **bat**. (Repeat **bat**.) Say **bat**. (Repeat **bat**.) Say **bat** without the /b/.　　　*(/at/)*

Say **sat**. (Repeat **sat**.) Say **sat**. (Repeat **sat**.) Say **sat** without the /s/.　　　*(/at/)*

Say **pal**. (Repeat **pal**.) Say **pal**. (Repeat **pal**.) Say **pal** without the /p/.　　　*(/al/)*

Say **nap**. (Repeat **nap**.) Say **nap**. (Repeat **nap**.) Say **nap** without the /n/.　　　*(/ap/)*

Stage 7: Phoneme Substitution

Say **rap**. (Repeat **rap**.) Say **rap**. (Repeat **rap**.) Now, change the first sound in **rap** to /l/.　　　(lap)

Say **lap**. (Repeat **lap**.) Say **lap**. (Repeat **lap**.) Now, change the first sound in **lap** to /t/.　　　(tap)

Say **can**. (Repeat **can**.) Say **can**. (Repeat **can**.) Now, change the first sound in **can** to /t/.　　　(tan)

Say **jam**. (Repeat **jam**.) Say **jam**. (Repeat **jam**.) Now, change the first sound in **jam** to /h/.　　　(ham)

Say **nap**. (Repeat **nap**.) Say **nap**. (Repeat **nap**.) Now, change the first sound in **nap** to /k/.　　　(cap)

Say **lab**. (Repeat **lab**.) Say **lab**. (Repeat **lab**.) Now, change the first sound in **lab** to /k/.　　　(cab)

Advancement: After initial phoneme(s), substitute final phoneme(s):

Say **hat**. (Repeat **hat**.) Say **hat**. (Repeat **hat**.) Now, change the last sound in **hat** to /m/.　　　(ham)

Say **bam**. (Repeat **bam**.) Say **bam**. (Repeat **bam**.) Now, change the last sound in **bam** to /t/.　　　(bat)

Say **cam**. (Repeat **cam**.) Say **cam**. (Repeat **cam**.) Now, change the last sound in **cam** to /b/. (cab)

Say **fab**. (Repeat **fab**.) Say **fab**. (Repeat **fab**.) Now, change the last sound in **fab** to /t/.   (fat)

Say **bat**. (Repeat **bat**.) Say **bat**. (Repeat **bat**.) Now, change the last sound in **bat** to /m/.   (bam)

Say **tab**. (Repeat **tab**.) Say **tab**. (Repeat **tab**.) Now, change the last sound in **tab** to /m/.   (tam)

Say **ham**. (Repeat **ham**.) Say **ham**. (Repeat **ham**.) Now, change the last sound in **ham** to /t/.   (hat)

Stage 8: Phoneme Reversal

Say **mat**. (Repeat **mat**.) Say **mat**. (Repeat **mat**.)
Now, change the first sound to last, and the last sound to first.   (tam)

Say **bad**. (Repeat **bad**.) Say **bad**. (Repeat **bad**.)
Now, change the first sound to last, and the last sound to first.   (dab)

Say **tab**. (Repeat **tab**.) Say **tab**. (Repeat **tab**.)
Now, change the first sound to last, and the last sound to first.   (bat)

Say **Mac**. (Repeat **Mac**.) Say **Mac**. (Repeat **Mac**.)
Now, change the first sound to last, and the last sound to first.   (cam)

Say **tam**. (Repeat **tam**.) Say **tam**. (Repeat **tam**.)
Now, change the first sound to last, and the last sound to first.   (mat)

Say **bat**. (Repeat **bat**.) Say **bat**. (Repeat **bat**.)
Now, change the first sound to last, and the last sound to first.   (tab)

Stage 9: Pig Latin

Three or four modelings may be necessary with this activity, particularly for students with a significant lack of phonemic awareness. Do not penalize students who cannot master Pig Latin.

Say **jam**. (Repeat **jam**.) Say **jam**. (Repeat **jam**.) Say **jam** without the /j/.   (/am/)

Say /am/. (Repeat /am/.) Say /am/. (Repeat /am/.) Say /am/ with /j/ at the end.   (/am j/)

Now, say /ay/ at the end.   (/am jay/)

Say **rat**. (Repeat **rat**.) Say **rat**. (Repeat **rat**.) Say **rat** without the /r/.   (/at/)

Say /at/. (Repeat /at/.) Say /at/. (Repeat /at/.) Say /at/ with /r/ at the end.   (/at r/)

Now, say /ay/ at the end.   (/at ray/)

Say **sat**. (Repeat **sat**.) Say **sat**. (Repeat **sat**.) Say **sat** without the /s/.   (/at/)

Say /at/. (Repeat /at/.) Say /at/. (Repeat /at/.) Say /at/ with /s/ at the end.   (/at s/)

Now, say /ay/ at the end.   (/at say/)

Say **lap**. (Repeat **lap**.) Say **lap**. (Repeat **lap**.) Say **lap** without the /l/.   (/ap/)

Say /ap/. (Repeat /ap/.) Say /ap/. (Repeat /ap/.) Say /ap/ with /l/ at the end.   (/ap l/)

Now, say /ay/ at the end.   (/ap lay/)

Now, say together in Pig Latin: "I can speak Pig Latin."   (Iay ancay eakspay igpay atinlay)

Reading/Spelling Vocabulary

Al	hat	map	pat	tap
as	jab	nab	ram	*the*
can	jam	nap	ran	
fan	lab	Nat	rap	
ham	lap	pal	rat	
has	man	pan	tan	

Unit 3

Phonemic Awareness Drills

These sequential, cumulative drills assess and build phonemic awareness in emerging readers and spellers. To initiate daily lessons, present portions of these drills orally—without corresponding letters. Phonemes (sounds) should be mastered before they are associated with their orthographic representations (letters). After phonemic awareness has been established for a unit's new phonology concepts, students can be introduced to the unit's new symbol-sound correspondences and its reading/spelling vocabulary.

Phonology Concepts for Unit 3:

A phoneme is a sound. A grapheme is a letter.

- Consonant phonemes are closed sounds:

  - Review: /t /, /s/, /m/, /b/, /k/, /f/, /r/, /h/, /j/, /n/, /l/, /p/

  - New: /g/, /d/, /v/

- Vowel phonemes are open sounds. Review: short /a/

- Every word has a vowel phoneme.

- Sound-letter (phoneme-grapheme) relationships:

  - Review: **t**, **s**, **m**, **b**, **c**, **f**, **r**, **h**, **j**, **n**, **l**, **p**

  - New: **g**, **d**, **v**

Stage 1: Phoneme Production/Replication

Have the students repeat each isolated phoneme:

- Repeat these sounds:

/a/	/t/	/s/	/m/	/b/	/k/	/f/	/r/	/h/	/j/	/n/	/l/	/p/
am	tan	sat	mat	bat	cat	fat	ran	hat	jab	nab	lap	pat

- Repeat these new sounds:

/g/	/d/	/v/
gap	dad	van

Stage 2: Phoneme Isolation

Say **ad**. (Repeat **ad**.) Say **ad**. (Repeat **ad**.) What's the first sound in **ad**?   (/a/) (short **a**)

Say **had**. (Repeat **had**.) Say **had**. (Repeat **had**.) What's the last sound in **had**?   (/d/)

Say **gab**. (Repeat **gab**.) Say **gab**. (Repeat **gab**.) What's the first sound in **gab**?   (/g/)

Say **dab**. (Repeat **dab**.) Say **dab**. (Repeat **dab**.) What's the first sound in **dab**?   (/d/)

Say **pad**. (Repeat **pad**.) Say **pad**. (Repeat **pad**.) What's the last sound in **pad**?   (/d/)

Say **van**. (Repeat **van**.) Say **van**. (Repeat **van**.) What's the middle sound in **van**?   (/a/) (short **a**)

Say **van**. (Repeat **van**.) Say **van**. (Repeat **van**.) What's the first sound in **van**?   (/v/)

Say **bag**. (Repeat **bag**.) Say **bag**. (Repeat **bag**.) What's the last sound in **bag**?   (/g/)

Say **lap**. (Repeat **lap**.) Say **lap**. (Repeat **lap**.) What's the middle sound in **lap**?   (/a/) (short **a**)

Say **lad**. (Repeat **lad**.) Say **lad**. (Repeat **lad**.) What's the first sound in **lad**?   (/l/)

Say **fad**. (Repeat **fad**.) Say **fad**. (Repeat **fad**.) What's the middle sound in **fad**?   (/a/) (short **a**)

Say **jag**. (Repeat **jag**.) Say **jag**. (Repeat **jag**.) What's the last sound in **jag**?   (/g/)

Say **jag**. (Repeat **jag**.) Say **jag**. (Repeat **jag**.) What's the first sound in **jag**?   (/j/)

Say **gap**. (Repeat **gap**.) Say **gap**. (Repeat **gap**.) What's the first sound in **gap**?   (/g/)

Stage 3: Phoneme Segmentation and Counting (Spelling the Sounds)

Say **dad**. (Repeat **dad**.) Say **dad**. (Repeat **dad**.) Say the sounds in **dad**.   (/d/ /a/ /d/)

Say **gap**. (Repeat **gap**.) Say **gap**. (Repeat **gap**.) Say the sounds in **gap**.   (/g/ /a/ /p/)

Say **van**. (Repeat **van**.) Say **van**. (Repeat **van**.) Say the sounds in **van**.   (/v/ /a/ /n/)

Say **ad**. (Repeat **ad**.) Say **ad**. (Repeat **ad**.) Say the sounds in **ad**.   (/a/ /d/)

Say **jag**. (Repeat **jag**.) Say **jag**. (Repeat **jag**.) Say the sounds in **jag**.   (/j/ /a/ /g/)

Say **bag**. (Repeat **bag**.) Say **bag**. (Repeat **bag**.) Say the sounds in **bag**.   (/b/ /a/ /g/)

Say **had**. (Repeat **had**.) Say **had**. (Repeat **had**.) Say the sounds in **had**.   (/h/ /a/ /d/)

Say **an**. (Repeat **an**.) Say **an**. (Repeat **an**.) Say the sounds in **an**.   (/a/ /n/)

Say **pad**. (Repeat **pad**.) Say **pad**. (Repeat **pad**.) Say the sounds in **pad**.   (/p/ /a/ /d/)

Say **vat**. (Repeat **vat**.) Say **vat**. (Repeat **vat**.) Say the sounds in **vat**.   (/v/ /a/ /t/)

Say **pal**. (Repeat **pal**.) Say **pal**. (Repeat **pal**.) Say the sounds in **pal**.   (/p/ /a/ /l/)

After the students have been introduced to the new unit's vocabulary words, you may ask, "How many sounds in **xxx**?" "How many letters in **xxx**?"

Stage 4: Phoneme Blending

Listen and repeat. Listen and repeat: /a/ /d/. (Repeat phoneme series three times.)   (ad)

Listen and repeat. Listen and repeat: /b/ /a/ /g/. (Repeat phoneme series three times.)   (bag)

Listen and repeat. Listen and repeat: /v/ /a/ /n/. (Repeat phoneme series three times.)   (van)

Listen and repeat. Listen and repeat: /h/ /a/ /d/. (Repeat phoneme series three times.)   (had)

Listen and repeat. Listen and repeat: /r/ /a/ /d/. (Repeat phoneme series three times.)   (rad)

Listen and repeat. Listen and repeat: /t/ /a/ /g/. (Repeat phoneme series three times.)   (tag)

Listen and repeat. Listen and repeat: /v/ /a/ /t/. (Repeat phoneme series three times.)   (vat)

Listen and repeat. Listen and repeat: /s/ /a/ /g/. (Repeat phoneme series three times.)   (sag)

Listen and repeat. Listen and repeat: /l/ /a/ /g/. (Repeat phoneme series three times.)   (lag)

Stage 5: Rhyming

Say **rag**. (Repeat **rag**.) Say **rag**. (Repeat **rag**.)
Say a word that rhymes with **rag**.   (tag, bag, hag, lag)

Say **vat**. (Repeat **vat**.) Say **vat**. (Repeat **vat**.)
Say a word that rhymes with **vat**.   (hat, mat, rat, bat)

Say **had**. (Repeat **had**.) Say **had**. (Repeat **had**.)
Say a word that rhymes with **had**.   (dad, mad, pad, sad)

Say **bag**. (Repeat **bag**.) Say **bag**. (Repeat **bag**.)
Say a word that rhymes with **bag**.   (rag, lag, nag, hag)

Say **nap**. (Repeat **nap**.) Say **nap**. (Repeat **nap**.)
Say a word that rhymes with **nap**.   (rap, cap, lap, tap)

Say **gap**. (Repeat **gap**.) Say **gap**. (Repeat **gap**.)
Say a word that rhymes with **gap**.   (map, nap, cap, lap)

Say **van**. (Repeat **van**.) Say **van**. (Repeat **van**.)
Say a word that rhymes with **van**.   (man, tan, can, pan)

Say **gal**. (Repeat **gal**.) Say **gal**. (Repeat **gal**.)
Say a word that rhymes with **gal**.   (Al, pal, Hal, Sal)

Stage 6: Phoneme Deletion

Say **gap**. (Repeat **gap**.) Say **gap**. (Repeat **gap**.) Say **gap** without the /g/.   (/ap/)

Say **can**. (Repeat **can**.) Say **can**. (Repeat **can**.) Say **can** without the /k/.   (/an/)

Say **vat**. (Repeat **vat**.) Say **vat**. (Repeat **vat**.) Say **vat** without the /v/.   (/at/)

Say **lag**. (Repeat **lag**.) Say **lag**. (Repeat **lag**.) Say **lag** without the /l/.   (/ag/)

Say **have**. (Repeat **have**.) Say **have**. (Repeat **have**.) Say **have** without the /v/.   (/ha/)

Say **mad**. (Repeat **mad**.) Say **mad**. (Repeat **mad**.) Say **mad** without the /m/.   (/ad/)

Say **van**. (Repeat **van**.) Say **van**. (Repeat **van**.) Say **van** without the /n/.   (/va/)

Say **pad**. (Repeat **pad**.) Say **pad**. (Repeat **pad**.) Say **pad** without the /p/.   (/ad/)

Say **rag**. (Repeat **rag**.) Say **rag**. (Repeat **rag**.) Say **rag** without the /g/.   (/ra/)

Say **lag**. (Repeat **lag**.) Say **lag**. (Repeat **lag**.) Say **lag** without the /l/.   (/ag/)

Say **pal**. (Repeat **pal**.) Say **pal**. (Repeat **pal**.) Say **pal** without the /p/.   (/al/)

Say **dab**. (Repeat **dab**.) Say **dab**. (Repeat **dab**.) Say **dab** without the /b/.   (/da/)

Stage 7: Phoneme Substitution

Say **rap**. (Repeat **rap**.) Say **rap**. (Repeat **rap**.) Now, change the first sound in **rap** to /l/.   (lap)

Say **mad**. (Repeat **mad**.) Say **mad**. (Repeat **mad**.) Now, change the first sound in **mad** to /d/. (dad)

Say **van**. (Repeat **van**.) Say **van**. (Repeat **van**.) Now, change the first sound in **van** to /t/.   (tan)

Say **can**. (Repeat **can**.) Say **can**. (Repeat **can**.) Now, change the first sound in **can** to /v/.   (van)

Say **gap**. (Repeat **gap**.) Say **gap**. (Repeat **gap**.) Now, change the first sound in **gap** to /n/.   (nap)

Say **lab**. (Repeat **lab**.) Say **lab**. (Repeat **lab**.) Now, change the first sound in **lab** to /g/.   (gab)

Advancement: After initial phoneme(s), substitute final phoneme(s):

Say **tag**. (Repeat **tag**.) Say **tag**. (Repeat **tag**.) Now, change the last sound in **tag** to /m/.   (tam)

Say **gab**. (Repeat **gab**.) Say **gab**. (Repeat **gab**.) Now, change the last sound in **gab** to /s/.   (gas)

Say **vat**. (Repeat **vat**.) Say **vat**. (Repeat **vat**.) Now, change the last sound in **vat** to /n/.   (van)

Say **sad**. (Repeat **sad**.) Say **sad**. (Repeat **sad**.) Now, change the last sound in **sad** to /t/.   (sat)

Say **bag**. (Repeat **bag**.) Say **bag**. (Repeat **bag**.) Now, change the last sound in **bag** to /d/.   (bad)

Say **dad**. (Repeat **dad**.) Say **dad**. (Repeat **dad**.) Now, change the last sound in **dad** to /n/.   (Dan)

Say **gap**. (Repeat **gap**.) Say **gap**. (Repeat **gap**.) Now, change the last sound in **gap** to /l/.   (gal)

Stage 8: Phoneme Reversal

Say **bag**. (Repeat **bag**.) Say **bag**. (Repeat **bag**.)
Now, change the first sound to last, and the last sound to first.   (gab)

Say **bad**. (Repeat **bad**.) Say **bad**. (Repeat **bad**.)
Now, change the first sound to last, and the last sound to first.   (dab)

Say **tab**. (Repeat **tab**.) Say **tab**. (Repeat **tab**.)
Now, change the first sound to last, and the last sound to first.   (bat)

Say **ban**. (Repeat **ban**.) Say **ban**. (Repeat **ban**.)
Now, change the first sound to last, and the last sound to first.   (nab)

Say **bat**. (Repeat **bat**.) Say **bat**. (Repeat **bat**.)
Now, change the first sound to last, and the last sound to first.   (tab)

Say **pass**. (Repeat **pass**.) Say **pass**. (Repeat **pass**.)
Now, change the first sound to last, and the last sound to first.   (sap)

Stage 9: Pig Latin

Three or four modelings may be necessary with this activity, particularly for students with a significant lack of phonemic awareness. Do not penalize students who cannot master Pig Latin.

Say **van**. (Repeat **van**.) Say **van**. (Repeat **van**.) Say **van** without the /*v*/.   (/*an*/)

Say /*an*/. (Repeat /*an*/.) Say /*an*/. (Repeat /*an*/.) Say /*an*/ with /*v*/ at the end.   (/*an v*/)

Now, say /*ay*/ at the end.   (/*an vay*/)

Say **rag**. (Repeat **rag**.) Say **rag**. (Repeat **rag**.) Say **rag** without the /*r*/.   (/*ag*/)

Say /*ag*/. (Repeat /*ag*/.) Say /*ag*/. (Repeat /*ag*/.) Say /*ag*/ with /*r*/ at the end.   (/*ag r*/)

Now, say /*ay*/ at the end.   (/*ag ray*/)

Say **lad**. (Repeat **lad**.) Say **lad**. (Repeat **lad**.) Say **lad** without the /*l*/.   (/*ad*/)

Say /*ad*/. (Repeat /*ad*/.) Say /*ad*/. (Repeat /*ad*/.) Say /*ad*/ with /*l*/ at the end.   (/*ad l*/)

Now, say /*ay*/ at the end.   (/*ad lay*/)

Say **gap**. (Repeat **gap**.) Say **gap**. (Repeat **gap**.) Say **gap** without the /*g*/.   (/*ap*/)

Say /*ap*/. (Repeat /*ap*/.) Say /*ap*/. (Repeat /*ap*/.) Say /*ap*/ with /*g*/ at the end.   (/*ap g*/)

Now, say /*ay*/ at the end.   (/*ap gay*/)

Now, say together in Pig Latin: "I can speak Pig Latin."   (Iay ancay eakspay igpay atinlay)

Reading/Spelling Vocabulary

bad	gas	lap	sad	*to*
bag	had	mad	sag	
dad	lab	pad	tag	
dam	lad	Pam	van	
gal	lag	rag	vat	

Unit 4

Phonemic Awareness Drills

These sequential, cumulative drills assess and build phonemic awareness in emerging readers and spellers. To initiate daily lessons, present portions of these drills orally—without corresponding letters. Phonemes (sounds) should be mastered before they are associated with their orthographic representations (letters). After phonemic awareness has been established for a unit's new phonology concepts, students can be introduced to the unit's new symbol-sound correspondences and its reading/spelling vocabulary.

Phonology Concepts for Unit 4

A phoneme is a sound. A grapheme is a letter.

- Consonant phonemes are closed sounds:

  - Review: /t/, /s/, /m/, /b/, /k/, /f/, /r/, /h/, /j/, /n/, /l/, /p/, /g/, /d/, /v/

  - New: /w/

- Vowel phonemes are open sounds.

  - Review: short /a/

  - New: short /i/

- Every word has a vowel phoneme.

- Sound-letter (phoneme-grapheme) relationships:

  - Review: <u>a</u>, <u>t</u>, <u>s</u>, <u>m</u>, <u>b</u>, <u>c</u>, <u>f</u>, <u>r</u>, <u>h</u>, <u>j</u>, <u>n</u>, <u>l</u>, <u>p</u>, <u>g</u>, <u>d</u>, <u>v</u>

  - New: <u>w</u>, <u>i</u>

Stage 1: Phoneme Production/Replication

Have the students repeat each isolated phoneme:

- Repeat these sounds:

/a/	/t/	/s/	/m/	/b/	/k/	/f/	/r/	/h/	/j/	/n/	/l/	/p/	/g/	/d/	/v/
am	tan	sat	mat	bat	cat	fat	ran	hat	jab	nab	lap	pat	gap	dad	van

- Repeat these new sounds:

/i/	/w/
it	wag

Stage 2: Phoneme Isolation

Say **wag**. (Repeat **wag**.) Say **wag**. (Repeat **wag**.) What's the first sound in **wag**?   (/w/)

Say **wag**. (Repeat **wag**.) Say **wag**. (Repeat **wag**.) What's the middle sound in **wag**? (/a/) (short **a**)

Say **dip**. (Repeat **dip**.) Say **dip**. (Repeat **dip**.) What's the last sound in **dip**?   (/p/)

Say **gap**. (Repeat **gap**.) Say **gap**. (Repeat **gap**.) What's the first sound in **gap**?   (/g/)

Say **him**. (Repeat **him**.) Say **him**. (Repeat **him**.) What's the first sound in **him**?   (/h/)

Say **him**. (Repeat **him**.) Say **him**. (Repeat **him**.) What's the last sound in **him**?   (/m/)

Say **wig**. (Repeat **wig**.) Say **wig**. (Repeat **wig**.) What's the middle sound in **wig**?   (/i/) (short **i**)

Say **rim**. (Repeat **rim**.) Say **rim**. (Repeat **rim**.) What's the first sound in **rim**?   (/r/)

Say **pig**. (Repeat **pig**.) Say **pig**. (Repeat **pig**.) What's the last sound in **pig**?   (/g/)

Say **lip**. (Repeat **lip**.) Say **lip**. (Repeat **lip**.) What's the middle sound in **lip**?   (/i/) (short **i**)

Say **wig**. (Repeat **wig**.) Say **wig**. (Repeat **wig**.) What's the first sound in **wig**?   (/w/)

Stage 3: Phoneme Segmentation and Counting (Spelling the Sounds)

Say **wig**. (Repeat **wig**.) Say **wig**. (Repeat **wig**.) Say the sounds in **wig**.   (/w/ /i/ /g/)

Say **pin**. (Repeat **pin**.) Say **pin**. (Repeat **pin**.) Say the sounds in **pin**.   (/p/ /i/ /n/)

Say **rid**. (Repeat **rid**.) Say **rid**. (Repeat **rid**.) Say the sounds in **rid**.   (/r/ /i/ /d/)

Say **ad**. (Repeat **ad**.) Say **ad**. (Repeat **ad**.) Say the sounds in **ad**.   (/a/ /d/)

Say **jag**. (Repeat **jag**.) Say **jag**. (Repeat **jag**.) Say the sounds in **jag**.   (/j/ /a/ /g/)

Say **bag**. (Repeat **bag**.) Say **bag**. (Repeat **bag**.) Say the sounds in **bag**.   (/b/ /a/ /g/)

Say **had**. (Repeat **had**.) Say **had**. (Repeat **had**.) Say the sounds in **had**.   (/h/ /a/ /d/)

Say **at**. (Repeat **at**.) Say **at**. (Repeat **at**.) Say the sounds in **at**.   (/a/ /t/)

Say **pad**. (Repeat **pad**.) Say **pad**. (Repeat **pad**.) Say the sounds in **pad**.   (/p/ /a/ /d/)

Say **vat**. (Repeat **vat**.) Say **vat**. (Repeat **vat**.) Say the sounds in **vat**.   (/v/ /a/ /t/)

Say **pal**. (Repeat **pal**.) Say **pal**. (Repeat **pal**.) Say the sounds in **pal**.   (/p/ /a/ /l/)

Stage 4: Phoneme Blending

Listen and repeat. Listen and repeat: /i/ /n/. (Repeat phoneme series three times.)   (in)

Listen and repeat. Listen and repeat: /b/ /i/ /g/. (Repeat phoneme series three times.)   (big)

Listen and repeat. Listen and repeat: /v/ /a/ /n/. (Repeat phoneme series three times.)   (van)

Listen and repeat. Listen and repeat: /h/ /i/ /d/. (Repeat phoneme series three times.)   (hid)

Listen and repeat. Listen and repeat: /r/ /i/ /d/. (Repeat phoneme series three times.)   (rid)

Listen and repeat. Listen and repeat: /t/ /a/ /g/. (Repeat phoneme series three times.)   (tag)

Listen and repeat. Listen and repeat: /b/ /i/ /n/. (Repeat phoneme series three times.)   (bin)

Listen and repeat. Listen and repeat: /s/ /a/ /g/. (Repeat phoneme series three times.)   (sag)

Listen and repeat. Listen and repeat: /r/ /i/ /p/. (Repeat phoneme series three times.)   (rip)

Stage 5: Rhyming

Say **bit**. (Repeat **bit**.) Say **bit**. (Repeat **bit**.)
Say a word that rhymes with **bit**.   (hit, sit, lit)

Say **lid**. (Repeat **lid**.) Say **lid**. (Repeat **lid**.)
Say a word that rhymes with **lid**.   (bid, kid, did)

Say **rig**. (Repeat **rig**.) Say **rig**. (Repeat **rig**.)
Say a word that rhymes with **rig**.   (big, pig, dig)

Say **bag**. (Repeat **bag**.) Say **bag**. (Repeat **bag**.)
Say a word that rhymes with **bag**.   (rag, lag, nag)

Say **nap**. (Repeat **nap**.) Say **nap**. (Repeat **nap**.)
Say a word that rhymes with **nap**.   (rap, cap, lap)

Say **gap**. (Repeat **gap**.) Say **gap**. (Repeat **gap**.)
Say a word that rhymes with **gap**.   (map, nap, cap)

Say **win**. (Repeat **win**.) Say **win**. (Repeat **win**.)
Say a word that rhymes with **win**.   (din, fin, pin)

Say **gal**. (Repeat **gal**.) Say **gal**. (Repeat **gal**.)
Say a word that rhymes with **gal**.   (Al, pal, Hal)

Stage 6: Phoneme Deletion

Say **gap**. (Repeat **gap**.) Say **gap**. (Repeat **gap**.) Say **gap** without the /g/.   (/ap/)

Say **rag**. (Repeat **rag**.) Say **rag**. (Repeat **rag**.) Say **rag** without the /r/.   (/ag/)

Say **rig**. (Repeat **rig**.) Say **rig**. (Repeat **rig**.) Say **rig** without the /r/.   (/ig/)

Say **lit**. (Repeat **lit**.) Say **lit**. (Repeat **lit**.) Say **lit** without the /l/.   (/it/)

Say **lag**. (Repeat **lag**.) Say **lag**. (Repeat **lag**.) Say **lag** without the /l/.   (/ag/)

Say **him**. (Repeat **him**.) Say **him**. (Repeat **him**.) Say **him** without the /h/.　　　(/im/)

Say **van**. (Repeat **van**.) Say **van**. (Repeat **van**.) Say **van** without the /n/.　　　(/va/)

Say **had**. (Repeat **had**.) Say **had**. (Repeat **had**.) Say **had** without the /d/.　　　(/ha/)

Say **rat**. (Repeat **rat**.) Say **rat**. (Repeat **rat**.) Say **rat** without the /t/.　　　(/ra/)

Say **tag**. (Repeat **tag**.) Say **tag**. (Repeat **tag**.) Say **tag** without the /g/.　　　(/ta/)

Say **pig**. (Repeat **pig**.) Say **pig**. (Repeat **pig**.) Say **pig** without the /p/.　　　(/ig/)

Say **dim**. (Repeat **dim**.) Say **dim**. (Repeat **dim**.) Say **dim** without the /d/.　　　(/im/)

Stage 7: Phoneme Substitution

Say **rig**. (Repeat **rig**.) Say **rig**. (Repeat **rig**.) Now, change the first sound in **rig** to /p/.　　(pig)

Say **mad**. (Repeat **mad**.) Say **mad**. (Repeat **mad**.) Now, change the first sound in **mad** to /h/. (had)

Say **hit**. (Repeat **hit**.) Say **hit**. (Repeat **hit**.) Now, change the first sound in **hit** to /p/.　　(pit)

Say **lit**. (Repeat **lit**.) Say **lit**. (Repeat **lit**.) Now, change the first sound in **lit** to /h/.　　(hit)

Say **man**. (Repeat **man**.) Say **man**. (Repeat **man**.) Now, change the first sound in **man** to /v/. (van)

Say **him**. (Repeat **him**.) Say **him**. (Repeat **him**.) Now, change the first sound in **him** to /d/. (dim)

Advancement: After initial phoneme(s), substitute final phoneme(s) and medial phoneme(s):

Say **hit**. (Repeat **hit**.) Say **hit**. (Repeat **hit**.) Now, change the last sound in **hit** to /m/.　　(him)

Say **hit**. (Repeat **hit**.) Say **hit**. (Repeat **hit**.) Now, change the last sound in **hit** to /p/.　　(hip)

Say **rig**. (Repeat **rig**.) Say **rig**. (Repeat **rig**.) Now, change the last sound in **rig** to /m/.　　(rim)

Say **dim**. (Repeat **dim**.) Say **dim**. (Repeat **dim**.) Now, change the last sound in **dim** to /g/.　(dig)

Say **big**. (Repeat **big**.) Say **big**. (Repeat **big**.) Now, change the middle sound in **big** to /a/. (bag)

Say **gag**. (Repeat **gag**.) Say **gag**. (Repeat **gag**.) Now, change the last sound in **gag** to /p/.　(gap)

Say **will**. (Repeat **will**.) Say **will**. (Repeat **will**.) Now, change the last sound in **will** to /g/. (wig)

Say **rig**. (Repeat **rig**.) Say **rig**. (Repeat **rig**.) Now, change the middle sound in **rig** to /a/. (rag)

Say **Jim**. (Repeat **Jim**.) Say **Jim**. (Repeat **Jim**.) Now, change the last sound in **Jim** to /g/.　(jig)

Say **pill**. (Repeat **pill**.) Say **pill**. (Repeat **pill**.) Now, change the last sound in **pill** to /n/.　(pin)

Say **have**. (Repeat **have**.) Say **have**. (Repeat **have**.) Now, change the last sound in **have** to /m/. (ham)

Say **did**. (Repeat **did**.) Say **did**. (Repeat **did**.) Now, change the middle sound in **did** to /a/. (dad)

Stage 8: Phoneme Reversal

Say **dill**. (Repeat **dill**.) Say **dill**. (Repeat **dill**.)
Now, change the first sound to last, and the last sound to first.   (lid)

Say **pin**. (Repeat **pin**.) Say **pin**. (Repeat **pin**.)
Now, change the first sound to last, and the last sound to first.   (nip)

Say **tap**. (Repeat **tap**.) Say **tap**. (Repeat **tap**.)
Now, change the first sound to last, and the last sound to first.   (pat)

Say **mid**. (Repeat **mid**.) Say **mid**. (Repeat **mid**.)
Now, change the first sound to last, and the last sound to first.   (dim)

Say **bag**. (Repeat **bag**.) Say **bag**. (Repeat **bag**.)
Now, change the first sound to last, and the last sound to first.   (gab)

Say **Tim**. (Repeat **Tim**.) Say **Tim**. (Repeat **Tim**.)
Now, change the first sound to last, and the last sound to first.   (mit)

Say **pill**. (Repeat **pill**.) Say **pill**. (Repeat **pill**.)
Now, change the first sound to last, and the last sound to first.   (lip)

Stage 9: Pig Latin

Three or four modelings may be necessary with this activity, particularly for students with a significant lack of phonemic awareness. Do not penalize students who cannot master Pig Latin.

Say **wig**. (Repeat **wig**.) Say **wig**. (Repeat **wig**.) Say **wig** without the /*w*/.   (/*ig*/)

Say /*ig*/. (Repeat /*ig*/.) Say /*ig*/. (Repeat /*ig*/.) Say /*ig*/ with /*w*/ at the end.   (/*ig w*/)

Now, say /*ay*/ at the end.   (/*ig way*/)

Say **rag**. (Repeat **rag**.) Say **rag**. (Repeat **rag**.) Say **rag** without the /*r*/.   (/*ag*/)

Say /*ag*/. (Repeat /*ag*/.) Say /*ag*/. (Repeat /*ag*/.) Say /*ag*/ with /*r*/ at the end.   (/*ag r*/)

Now, say /*ay*/ at the end.   (/*ag ray*/)

Say **lag**. (Repeat **lag**.) Say **lag**. (Repeat **lag**.) Say **lag** without the /*l*/.   (/*ag*/)

Say /*ag*/. (Repeat /*ag*/.) Say /*ag*/. (Repeat /*ag*/.) Say /*ag*/ with /*l*/ at the end.   (/*ag l*/)

Now, say /*ay*/ at the end.   (/*ag lay*/)

Now, say together in Pig Latin: "I can speak Pig Latin."   (Iay ancay eakspay igpay atinlay)

Reading/Spelling Vocabulary

big	in	mit	tin
bit	is	pig	win
did	it	rig	wit
him	kid	rim	*have*
his	lid	rip	*I*
hit	Mac	sit	

Unit 5

Phonemic Awareness Drills

These sequential, cumulative drills assess and build phonemic awareness in emerging readers and spellers. To initiate daily lessons, present portions of these drills orally—without corresponding letters. Phonemes (sounds) should be mastered before they are associated with their orthographic representations (letters). After phonemic awareness has been established for a unit's new phonology concepts, students can be introduced to the unit's new symbol-sound correspondences and its reading/spelling vocabulary.

Phonology Concepts for Unit 5

A phoneme is a sound. A grapheme is a letter.

- Consonant phonemes are closed sounds:
  - Review: /t /, /s/, /m/, /b/, /k/, /f/, /g/, /d/, /r/, /h/, /j/, /n/, /l/, /p/, /v/, /w/

- Vowel phonemes are open sounds:
  - Review: short /a/, short /i/

- Every word has a vowel phoneme.

- Sound-letter (phoneme-grapheme) relationships:
  - Review: **t**, **s**, **m**, **b**, **c**, **f**, **r**, **h**, **j**, **n**, **l**, **p**, **g**, **d**, **v**, **w**
  - **c** can make the /k/ sound (phoneme). Review: **c**
  - **k** makes the /k/ sound (phoneme). New: **k**
  - **c** and **k** together make the /k/ sound (phoneme). New: **ck**

Stage 1: Phoneme Production/Replication

Have the students repeat each isolated phoneme:

Repeat these vowel sounds:

/a/	/i/
am	it

Repeat these consonant sounds:

/t/	/s/	/m/	/b/	/k/	/f/	/r/	/h/	/j/	/n/	/l/	/p/	/g/	/d/	/v/	/w/
tan	sat	mat	bat	cat	fat	ran	hat	jab	nab	lap	pat	gap	dad	van	wag

Repeat this new sound: /k/

/k/ is spelled three ways: <u>c</u>, <u>k</u>, <u>ck</u>.   (can, kit, kick)

Stage 2: Phoneme Isolation

Say **kick**. (Repeat **kick**.) Say **kick**. (Repeat **kick**.) What's the first sound in **kick**? (/k/)

Say **cap**. (Repeat **cap**.) Say **cap**. (Repeat **cap**.) What's the middle sound in **cap**?   (/a/) (short <u>a</u>)

Say **kid**. (Repeat **kid**.) Say **kid**. (Repeat **kid**.) What's the last sound in **kid**?   (/d/)

Say **Kim**. (Repeat **Kim**.) Say **Kim**. (Repeat **Kim**.) What's the first sound in **Kim**? (/k/)

Say **can**. (Repeat **can**.) Say **can**. (Repeat **can**.) What's the first sound in **can**?   (/k/)

Say **wag**. (Repeat **wag**.) Say **wag**. (Repeat **wag**.) What's the last sound in **wag**?   (/g/)

Say **wig**. (Repeat **wig**.) Say **wig**. (Repeat **wig**.) What's the middle sound in **wig**?   (/i/) (short <u>i</u>)

Say **tack**. (Repeat **tack**.) Say **tack**. (Repeat **tack**.) What's the first sound in **tack**?   (/t/)

Say **fig**. (Repeat **fig**.) Say **fig**. (Repeat **fig**.) What's the last sound in **fig**?   (/g/)

Say **tick**. (Repeat **tick**.) Say **tick**. (Repeat **tick**.) What's the middle sound in **tick**? (/i/) (short <u>i</u>)

Stage 3: Phoneme Segmentation and Counting (Spelling the Sounds)

Say **sick**. (Repeat **sick**.) Say **sick**. (Repeat **sick**.) Say the sounds in **sick**.   (/s/ /i/ /k/)

Say **wick**. (Repeat **wick**.) Say **wick**. (Repeat **wick**.) Say the sounds in **wick**.   (/w/ /i/ /k/)

Say **pack**. (Repeat **pack**.) Say **pack**. (Repeat **pack**.) Say the sounds in **pack**.   (/p/ /a/ /k/)

Say **rack**. (Repeat **rack**.) Say **rack**. (Repeat **rack**.) Say the sounds in **rack**.   (/r/ /a/ /k/)

Say **jag**. (Repeat **jag**.) Say **jag**. (Repeat **jag**.) Say the sounds in **jag**.   (/j/ /a/ /g/)

Say **kid**. (Repeat **kid**.) Say **kid**. (Repeat **kid**.) Say the sounds in **kid**.   (/k/ /i/ /d/)

Say **big**. (Repeat **big**.) Say **big**. (Repeat **big**.) Say the sounds in **big**.   (/b/ /i/ /g/)

Say **back**. (Repeat **back**.) Say **back**. (Repeat **back**.) Say the sounds in **back**.   (/b/ /a/ /k/)

Say **van**. (Repeat **van**.) Say **van**. (Repeat **van**.) Say the sounds in **van**.   (/v/ /a/ /n/)

Say **kick**. (Repeat **kick**.) Say **kick**. (Repeat **kick**.) Say the sounds in **kick**.   (/k/ /i/ /k/)

After the students have been introduced to the new unit's vocabulary words, you may ask, "How many sounds in **xxx**?" "How many letters in **xxx**?"

Stage 4: Phoneme Blending

Listen and repeat. Listen and repeat: /b/ /a/ /k/. (Repeat phoneme series three times.)   (back)

Listen and repeat. Listen and repeat: /k/ /i/ /k/. (Repeat phoneme series three times.)   (kick)

Listen and repeat. Listen and repeat: /k/ /a/ /p/. (Repeat phoneme series three times.)   (cap)

Listen and repeat. Listen and repeat: /p/ /i/ /k/. (Repeat phoneme series three times.)   (pick)

Listen and repeat. Listen and repeat: /t/ /a/ /k/. (Repeat phoneme series three times.)   (tack)

Listen and repeat. Listen and repeat: /t/ /a/ /g/. (Repeat phoneme series three times.)   (tag)

Listen and repeat. Listen and repeat: /l/ /i/ /k/. (Repeat phoneme series three times.)   (lick)

Listen and repeat. Listen and repeat: /r/ /a/ /g/. (Repeat phoneme series three times.)   (rag)

Listen and repeat. Listen and repeat: /r/ /a/ /k/. (Repeat phoneme series three times.)   (rack)

Stage 5: Rhyming

Say **sick**. (Repeat **sick**.) Say **sick**. (Repeat **sick**.)
Say a word that rhymes with **sick**.   (thick, tick, kick, lick)

Say **kid**. (Repeat **kid**.) Say **kid**. (Repeat **kid**.)
Say a word that rhymes with **kid**.   (rid, hid, did, lid)

Say **sack**. (Repeat **sack**.) Say **sack**. (Repeat **sack**.)
Say a word that rhymes with **sack**.   (pack, tack, back, lack)

Say **nip**. (Repeat **nip**.) Say **nip**. (Repeat **nip**.)
Say a word that rhymes with **nip**.   (sip, tip, lip, hip)

Say **bag**. (Repeat **bag**.) Say **bag**. (Repeat **bag**.)
Say a word that rhymes with **bag**.   (sag, tag, lag, gag)

Say **van**. (Repeat **van**.) Say **van**. (Repeat **van**.)
Say a word that rhymes with **van**.   (man, tan, can, pan)

Say **lack**. (Repeat **lack**.) Say **lack**. (Repeat **lack**.)
Say a word that rhymes with **lack**.   (hack, pack, tack, rack)

Stage 6: Phoneme Deletion

Say **sick**. (Repeat **sick**.) Say **sick**. (Repeat **sick**.) Say **sick** without the /s/.   (/ik/)

Say **pick**. (Repeat **pick**.) Say **pick**. (Repeat **pick**.) Say **pick** without the /p/.   (/ik/)

Say **sack**. (Repeat **sack**.) Say **sack**. (Repeat **sack**.) Say **sack** without the /k/.   (/sa/)

Say **rag**. (Repeat **rag**.) Say **rag**. (Repeat **rag**.) Say **rag** without the /r/.   (/ag/)

Say **sag**. (Repeat **sag**.) Say **sag**. (Repeat **sag**.) Say **sag** without the /s/.   (/ag/)

Say **rack**. (Repeat **rack**.) Say **rack**. (Repeat **rack**.) Say **rack** without the /r/.   (/ak/)

Say **bag**. (Repeat **bag**.) Say **bag**. (Repeat **bag**.) Say **bag** without the /b/.   (/ag/)

Say **cap**. (Repeat **cap**.) Say **cap**. (Repeat **cap**.) Say **cap** without the /k/.   (/ap/)

Say **back**. (Repeat **back**.) Say **back**. (Repeat **back**.) Say **back** without the /b/.   (/ak/)

Say **tack**. (Repeat **tack**.) Say **tack**. (Repeat **tack**.) Say **tack** without the /t/.   (/ak/)

Say **pig**. (Repeat **pig**.) Say **pig**. (Repeat **pig**.) Say **pig** without the /p/.   (/ig/)

Say **rig**. (Repeat **rig**.) Say **rig**. (Repeat **rig**.) Say **rig** without the /r/.   (/ig/)

Stage 7: Phoneme Substitution

Say **kick**. (Repeat **kick**.) Say **kick**. (Repeat **kick**.) Now, change the first sound in **kick** to /t/.   (tick)

Say **rig**. (Repeat **rig**.) Say **rig**. (Repeat **rig**.) Now, change the first sound in **rig** to /p/.   (pig)

Say **sack**. (Repeat **sack**.) Say **sack**. (Repeat **sack**.) Now, change the first sound in **sack** to /b/.   (back)

Say **cap**. (Repeat **cap**.) Say **cap**. (Repeat **cap**.) Now, change the first sound in **cap** to /g/.   (gap)

Say **tin**. (Repeat **tin**.) Say **tin**. (Repeat **tin**.) Now, change the first sound in **tin** to /w/.   (win)

Say **hid**. (Repeat **hid**.) Say **hid**. (Repeat **hid**.) Now, change the first sound in **hid** to /b/.   (bid)

Advancement: After initial phoneme(s), substitute final phoneme(s) and medial phoneme(s):

Say **back**. (Repeat **back**.) Say **back**. (Repeat **back**.) Now, change the last sound in **back** to /d/.   (bad)

Say **lip**. (Repeat **lip**.) Say **lip**. (Repeat **lip**.) Now, change the last sound in **lip** to /k/.   (lick)

Say **rig**. (Repeat **rig**.) Say **rig**. (Repeat **rig**.) Now, change the last sound in **rig** to /m/.   (rim)

Say **dim**. (Repeat **dim**.) Say **dim**. (Repeat **dim**.) Now, change the last sound in **dim** to /g/.   (dig)

Say **sick**. (Repeat **sick**.) Say **sick**. (Repeat **sick**.) Now, change the middle sound in **sick** to /a/. (sack)

Say **gag**. (Repeat **gag**.) Say **gag**. (Repeat **gag**.) Now, change the last sound in **gag** to /p/.   (gap)

Say **will**. (Repeat **will**.) Say **will**. (Repeat **will**.) Now, change the last sound in **will** to /g/.   (wig)

Say **sing**. (Repeat **sing**.) Say **sing**. (Repeat **sing**.) Now, change the middle sound in **sing** to /a/. (sang)

Say **Jack**. (Repeat **Jack**.) Say **Jack**. (Repeat **Jack**.) Now, change the last sound in **Jack** to /g/.   (jag)

Say **lit**. (Repeat **lit**.) Say **lit**. (Repeat **lit**.) Now, change the last sound in **lit** to /k/.   (lick)

Say **ham**. (Repeat **ham**.) Say **ham**. (Repeat **ham**.) Now, change the last sound in **ham** to /k/.   (hack)

Say **pick**. (Repeat **pick**.) Say **pick**. (Repeat **pick**.) Now, change the middle sound in **pick** to /a/. (pack)

Say **sack**. (Repeat **sack**.) Say **sack**. (Repeat **sack**.) Now, change the middle sound in **sack** to /i/. (sick)

Stage 8: Phoneme Reversal

Say **kiss**. (Repeat **kiss**.) Say **kiss**. (Repeat **kiss**.)
Now, change the first sound to last, and the last sound to first.   (sick)

Say **pin**. (Repeat **pin**.) Say **pin**. (Repeat **pin**.)
Now, change the first sound to last, and the last sound to first.   (nip)

Say **tap**. (Repeat **tap**.) Say **tap**. (Repeat **tap**.)
Now, change the first sound to last, and the last sound to first.   (pat)

Say **back**. (Repeat **back**.) Say **back**. (Repeat **back**.)
Now, change the first sound to last, and the last sound to first.   (cab)

Say **tick**. (Repeat **tick**.) Say **tick**. (Repeat **tick**.)
Now, change the first sound to last, and the last sound to first.   (kit)

Say **Nick**. (Repeat **Nick**.) Say **Nick**. (Repeat **Nick**.)
Now, change the first sound to last, and the last sound to first.   (kin)

Say **pack**. (Repeat **pack**.) Say **pack**. (Repeat **pack**.)
Now, change the first sound to last, and the last sound to first.   (cap)

Stage 9: Pig Latin

Three or four modelings may be necessary with this activity, particularly for students with a significant lack of phonemic awareness. Do not penalize students who cannot master Pig Latin.

Say **pick**. (Repeat **pick**.) Say **pick**. (Repeat **pick**.) Say **pick** without the /*p*/.   (/*ik*/)

Say /*ik*/. (Repeat /*ik*/.) Say /*ik*/. (Repeat /*ik*/.) Say /*ik*/ with /*p*/ at the end.   (/*ik p*/)

Now, say /*ay*/ at the end.   (/*ik pay*/)

Say **sack**. (Repeat **sack**.) Say **sack**. (Repeat **sack**.) Say **sack** without the /*s*/.   (/*ak*/)

Say /*ak*/. (Repeat /*ak*/.) Say /*ak*/. (Repeat /*ak*/.) Say /*ak*/ with /*s*/ at the end.   (/*ak s*/)

Now, say /*ay*/ at the end.   (/*ak say*/)

Say **sick**. (Repeat **sick**.) Say **sick**. (Repeat **sick**.) Say **sick** without the /*s*/.   (/*ik*/)

Say /*ik*/. (Repeat /*ik*/.) Say /*ik*/. (Repeat /*ik*/.) Say /*ik*/ with /*s*/ at the end.   (/*ik s*/)

Now, say /*ay*/ at the end.   (/*ik say*/)

Now, say together in Pig Latin: "I can speak Pig Latin."   (Iay ancay eakspay igpay atinlay)

Reading/Spelling Vocabulary

back	lack	Nick	rack	tack
hack	lick	pack	sack	*said*
kick	Mac	pick	sick	

Unit 6

Phonemic Awareness Drills

These sequential, cumulative drills assess and build phonemic awareness in emerging readers and spellers. To initiate daily lessons, present portions of these drills orally—without corresponding letters. Phonemes (sounds) should be mastered before they are associated with their orthographic representations (letters). After phonemic awareness has been established for a unit's new phonology concepts, students can be introduced to the unit's new symbol-sound correspondences and its reading/spelling vocabulary.

Phonology Concepts for Unit 6

A phoneme is a sound. A grapheme is a letter.

- Consonant phonemes are closed sounds:

  - Review: /t/, /s/, /m/, /b/, /k/, /f/, /g/, /d/, /r/, /h/, /j/, /n/, /l/, /p/, /v/, /w/

- Vowel phonemes are open sounds:

  - Review: short /a/, short /i/

- Every word has a vowel phoneme.

- Sound-letter (phoneme-grapheme) relationships:

  - Review: **t**, **s**, **m**, **b**, **c**, **f**, **r**, **h**, **j**, **n**, **l**, **p**, **g**, **d**, **v**, **w**

  - /k/ is sometimes spelled **-ck**.

  - New: /k/ is spelled **-ck** after a short vowel, at the end of a single-syllable word.

Stage 1: Phoneme Production/Replication

Have the students repeat each isolated phoneme:

- Repeat these vowel sounds:

  /a/   /i/
  am   it

- Repeat these consonant sounds:

/t/	/s/	/m/	/b/	/k/	/f/	/r/	/h/	/j/	/n/	/l/	/p/	/g/	/d/	/v/	/w/
tan	sat	mat	bat	cat	fat	ran	hat	jab	nab	lap	pat	gap	dad	van	wag

- Repeat this sound:

  /k/

  can   kit   kick

Spelling Rule: At the end of a single-syllable word, after a short vowel, the /k/ sound (phoneme) is spelled with two letters (graphemes): **-ck**.

Stage 2: Phoneme Isolation

Say **kick**. (Repeat **kick**.) Say **kick**. (Repeat **kick**.) What's the first sound in **kick**? (*/k/*)

Say **cap**. (Repeat **cap**.) Say **cap**. (Repeat **cap**.) What's the middle sound in **cap**? (*/a/*) (short **a**)

Say **bag**. (Repeat **bag**.) Say **bag**. (Repeat **bag**.) What's the last sound in **bag**? (*/g/*)

Say **kit**. (Repeat **kit**.) Say **kit**. (Repeat **kit**.) What's the first sound in **kit**? (*/k/*)

Say **can**. (Repeat **can**.) Say **can**. (Repeat **can**.) What's the first sound in **can**? (*/k/*)

Say **wag**. (Repeat **wag**.) Say **wag**. (Repeat **wag**.) What's the last sound in **wag**? (*/g/*)

Say **wig**. (Repeat **wig**.) Say **wig**. (Repeat **wig**.) What's the middle sound in **wig**? (*/i/*) (short **i**)

Say **tack**. (Repeat **tack**.) Say **tack**. (Repeat **tack**.) What's the first sound in **tack**? (*/t/*)

Say **fig**. (Repeat **fig**.) Say **fig**. (Repeat **fig**.) What's the last sound in **fig**? (*/g/*)

Say **tick**. (Repeat **tick**.) Say **tick**. (Repeat **tick**.) What's the middle sound in **tick**? (*/i/*) (short **i**)

Stage 3: Phoneme Segmentation and Counting (Spelling the Sounds)

Say **pick**. (Repeat **pick**.) Say **pick**. (Repeat **pick**.) Say the sounds in **pick**. (*/p/ /i/ /k/*)

Say **wig**. (Repeat **wig**.) Say **wig**. (Repeat **wig**.) Say the sounds in **wig**. (*/w/ /i/ /g/*)

Say **sack**. (Repeat **sack**.) Say **sack**. (Repeat **sack**.) Say the sounds in **sack**. (*/s/ /a/ /k/*)

Say **lick**. (Repeat **lick**.) Say **lick**. (Repeat **lick**.) Say the sounds in **lick**. (*/l/ /i/ /k/*)

Say **jam**. (Repeat **jam**.) Say **jam**. (Repeat **jam**.) Say the sounds in **jam**. (*/j/ /a/ /m/*)

Say **kid**. (Repeat **kid**.) Say **kid**. (Repeat **kid**.) Say the sounds in **kid**. (*/k/ /i/ /d/*)

Say **it**. (Repeat **it**.) Say **it**. (Repeat **it**.) Say the sounds in **it**. (*/i/ /t/*)

Say **tack**. (Repeat **tack**.) Say **tack**. (Repeat **tack**.) Say the sounds in **tack**. (*/t/ /a/ /k/*)

Say **gap**. (Repeat **gap**.) Say **gap**. (Repeat **gap**.) Say the sounds in **gap**. (*/g/ /a/ /p/*)

Say **lack**. (Repeat **lack**.) Say **lack**. (Repeat **lack**.) Say the sounds in **lack**. (*/l/ /a/ /k/*)

After the students have been introduced to the new unit's vocabulary words, you may ask, "How many sounds in **xxx**?" "How many letters in **xxx**?"

Stage 4: Phoneme Blending

Listen and repeat. Listen and repeat: /r/ /a/ /k/. (Repeat phoneme series three times.)   (rack)

Listen and repeat. Listen and repeat: /k/ /i/ /k/. (Repeat phoneme series three times.)   (kick)

Listen and repeat. Listen and repeat: /k/ /a/ /p/. (Repeat phoneme series three times.)   (cap)

Listen and repeat. Listen and repeat: /s/ /i/ /k/. (Repeat phoneme series three times.)   (sick)

Listen and repeat. Listen and repeat: /w/ /i/ /k/. (Repeat phoneme series three times.)   (wick)

Listen and repeat. Listen and repeat: /w/ /i/ /g/. (Repeat phoneme series three times.)   (wig)

Listen and repeat. Listen and repeat: /l/ /i/ /k/. (Repeat phoneme series three times.)   (lick)

Listen and repeat. Listen and repeat: /b/ /a/ /g/. (Repeat phoneme series three times.)   (bag)

Listen and repeat. Listen and repeat: /b/ /a/ /k/. (Repeat phoneme series three times.)   (back)

Stage 5: Rhyming

Say **wick**. (Repeat **wick**.) Say **wick**. (Repeat **wick**.)
Say a word that rhymes with **wick**.   (thick, tick, kick, lick)

Say **bid**. (Repeat **bid**.) Say **bid**. (Repeat **bid**.)
Say a word that rhymes with **bid**.   (rid, hid, did, lid)

Say **rack**. (Repeat **rack**.) Say **rack**. (Repeat **rack**.)
Say a word that rhymes with **rack**.   (pack, tack, back, lack)

Say **nag**. (Repeat **nag**.) Say **nag**. (Repeat **nag**.)
Say a word that rhymes with **nag**.   (sag, tag, lag, gag)

Say **bag**. (Repeat **bag**.) Say **bag**. (Repeat **bag**.)
Say a word that rhymes with **bag**.   (sag, tag, lag, gag)

Say **van**. (Repeat **van**.) Say **van**. (Repeat **van**.)
Say a word that rhymes with **van**.   (man, tan, can, pan)

Say **lack**. (Repeat **lack**.) Say **lack**. (Repeat **lack**.)
Say a word that rhymes with **lack**.   (hack, pack, tack, rack)

Stage 6: Phoneme Deletion

Say **sick**. (Repeat **sick**.) Say **sick**. (Repeat **sick**.) Say **sick** without the /s/.   (/ik/)

Say **pick**. (Repeat **pick**.) Say **pick**. (Repeat **pick**.) Say **pick** without the /p/.   (/ik/)

Say **sack**. (Repeat **sack**.) Say **sack**. (Repeat **sack**.) Say **sack** without the /k/.   (/sa/)

Say **rag**. (Repeat **rag**.) Say **rag**. (Repeat **rag**.) Say **rag** without the /r/.   (/ag/)

Say **sag**. (Repeat **sag**.) Say **sag**. (Repeat **sag**.) Say **sag** without the /s/. (/ag/)

Say **rack**. (Repeat **rack**.) Say **rack**. (Repeat **rack**.) Say **rack** without the /r/. (/ak/)

Say **bag**. (Repeat **bag**.) Say **bag**. (Repeat **bag**.) Say **bag** without the /b/. (/ag/)

Say **cap**. (Repeat **cap**.) Say **cap**. (Repeat **cap**.) Say **cap** without the /k/. (/ap/)

Say **back**. (Repeat **back**.) Say **back**. (Repeat **back**.) Say **back** without the /b/. (/ak/)

Say **tack**. (Repeat **tack**.) Say **tack**. (Repeat **tack**.) Say **tack** without the /t/. (/ak/)

Say **pig**. (Repeat **pig**.) Say **pig**. (Repeat **pig**.) Say **pig** without the /p/. (/ig/)

Say **rig**. (Repeat **rig**.) Say **rig**. (Repeat **rig**.) Say **rig** without the /r/. (/ig/)

Stage 7: Phoneme Substitution

Say **sack**. (Repeat **sack**.) Say **sack**. (Repeat **sack**.) Now, change the first sound in **sack** to /t/. (tack)

Say **big**. (Repeat **big**.) Say **big**. (Repeat **big**.) Now, change the first sound in **big** to /w/. (wig)

Say **back**. (Repeat **back**.) Say **back**. (Repeat **back**.) Now, change the first sound in **back** to /p/. (pack)

Say **Nick**. (Repeat **Nick**.) Say **Nick**. (Repeat **Nick**.) Now, change the first sound in **Nick** to /k/. (kick)

Say **tin**. (Repeat **tin**.) Say **tin**. (Repeat **tin**.) Now, change the first sound in **tin** to /w/. (win)

Say **hag**. (Repeat **hag**.) Say **hag**. (Repeat **hag**.) Now, change the first sound in **hag** to /w/. (wag)

Advancement: After initial phoneme(s), substitute final phoneme(s) and medial phoneme(s):

Say **back**. (Repeat **back**.) Say **back**. (Repeat **back**.) Now, change the last sound in **back** to /t/. (bat)

Say **lip**. (Repeat **lip**.) Say **lip**. (Repeat **lip**.) Now, change the last sound in **lip** to /k/. (lick)

Say **rig**. (Repeat **rig**.) Say **rig**. (Repeat **rig**.) Now, change the last sound in **rig** to /k/. (Rick)

Say **dim**. (Repeat **dim**.) Say **dim**. (Repeat **dim**.) Now, change the last sound in **dim** to /g/. (dig)

Say **sick**. (Repeat **sick**.) Say **sick**. (Repeat **sick**.) Now, change the middle sound in **sick** to /a/. (sack)

Say **gag**. (Repeat **gag**.) Say **gag**. (Repeat **gag**.) Now, change the last sound in **gag** to /p/. (gap)

Say **will**. (Repeat **will**.) Say **will**. (Repeat **will**.) Now, change the last sound in **will** to /g/. (wig)

Say **lack**. (Repeat **lack**.) Say **lack**. (Repeat **lack**.) Now, change the middle sound in **lack** to /i/. (lick)

Say **hick**. (Repeat **hick**.) Say **hick**. (Repeat **hick**.) Now, change the last sound in **hick** to /d/. (hid)

Say **tag**. (Repeat **tag**.) Say **tag**. (Repeat **tag**.) Now, change the last sound in **tag** to /k/. (tack)

Say **ham**. (Repeat **ham**.) Say **ham**. (Repeat **ham**.) Now, change the last sound in **ham** to /k/. (hack)

Say **pick**. (Repeat **pick**.) Say **pick**. (Repeat **pick**.) Now, change the middle sound in **pick** to /a/. (pack)

Say **sack**. (Repeat **sack**.) Say **sack**. (Repeat **sack**.) Now, change the middle sound in **sack** to /i/. (sick)

Stage 8: Phoneme Reversal

Say **cap**. (Repeat **cap**.) Say **cap**. (Repeat **cap**.)
Now, change the first sound to last, and the last sound to first.   (pack)

Say **kiss**. (Repeat **kiss**.) Say **kiss**. (Repeat **kiss**.)
Now, change the first sound to last, and the last sound to first.   (sick)

Say **cat**. (Repeat **cat**.) Say **cat**. (Repeat **cat**.)
Now, change the first sound to last, and the last sound to first.   (tack)

Say **pin**. (Repeat **pin**.) Say **pin**. (Repeat **pin**.)
Now, change the first sound to last, and the last sound to first.   (nip)

Say **kill**. (Repeat **kill**.) Say **kill**. (Repeat **kill**.)
Now, change the first sound to last, and the last sound to first.   (lick)

Say **ban**. (Repeat **ban**.) Say **ban**. (Repeat **ban**.)
Now, change the first sound to last, and the last sound to first.   (nab)

Say **cab**. (Repeat **cab**.) Say **cab**. (Repeat **cab**.)
Now, change the first sound to last, and the last sound to first.   (back)

Stage 9: Pig Latin

Three or four modelings may be necessary with this activity, particularly for students with a significant lack of phonemic awareness. Do not penalize students who cannot master Pig Latin.

Say **wick**. (Repeat **wick**.) Say **wick**. (Repeat **wick**.) Say **wick** without the /w/.   (/ik/)

Say /ik/. (Repeat /ik/.) Say /ik/. (Repeat /ik/.) Say /ik/ with /w/ at the end.   (/ik w/)

Now, say /ay/ at the end.   (/ik way/)

Say **back**. (Repeat **back**.) Say **back**. (Repeat **back**.) Now, say **back** without the /b/.   (/ak/)

Say /ak/. (Repeat /ak/.) Say /ak/. (Repeat /ak/.) Say /ak/ with /b/ at the end.   (/ak b/)

Now, say /ay/ at the end.   (/ak bay/)

Say **tag**. (Repeat **tag**.) Say **tag**. (Repeat **tag**.) Say **tag** without the /t/.   (/ag/)

Say /ag/. (Repeat /ag/.) Say /ag/. (Repeat /ag/.) Say /ag/ with /t/ at the end.   (/ag t/)

Now, say /ay/ at the end.   (/ag tay/)

Now, say together in Pig Latin: "I can speak Pig Latin."   (Iay ancay eakspay igpay atinlay)

Reading/Spelling Vocabulary

back	lick	Nick	Rat Pack	tack
hack	Mac	pack	Rick	*of*
kick	Mack	pick	sack	
lack	Mick	rack	sick	

Unit 7

Phonemic Awareness Drills

These sequential, cumulative drills assess and build phonemic awareness in emerging readers and spellers. To initiate daily lessons, present portions of these drills orally—without corresponding letters. Phonemes (sounds) should be mastered before they are associated with their orthographic representations (letters). After phonemic awareness has been established for a unit's new phonology concepts, students can be introduced to the unit's new symbol-sound correspondences and its reading/spelling vocabulary.

Phonology Concepts for Unit 7

- Consonant sounds (phonemes): Review: /b/, /d/, /f/, /g/, /h/, /j/, /k/, /l/, /m/, /n/, /p/, /r/, /s/, /t/, /v/, /w/

- Consonant letters (graphemes): Review: **b**, **c**, **d**, **f**, **g**, **h**, **j**, **k**, **l**, **m**, **n**, **p**, **r**, **s**, **t**, **v**, **w**

- Vowel sounds (phonemes): Review: short /a/, short /i/

- **qu** represents two phonemes: /kw/. (quick, quiz)

- **x** represents two phonemes: /ks/. (Max, fax)

- **y** represents /y/. (yak, yip)

- **z** represents /z/. (zap, zip)

- **s** sometimes represents /z/. (has, is)

Stage 1: Phoneme Production/Replication

Have the students repeat each isolated phoneme:

- Repeat these sounds:

  /a/ /i/
  am   it

- Repeat these consonant sounds:

/t/	/s/	/m/	/b/	/k/	/f/	/r/	/h/	/j/	/n/	/l/	/p/	/g/	/d/	/v/	/w/
tan	sat	mat	bat	cat	fat	ran	hat	jab	nab	lap	pat	gap	dad	van	wag

- Repeat these sounds:

/kw/	/ks/	/y/	/z/
quit	Max	yak	zip, is

Stage 2: Phoneme Isolation

Say **quick**. (Repeat **quick**.) Say **quick**. (Repeat **quick**.) What's the first sound in **quick**?	(/k/)
Say **ax**. (Repeat **ax**.) Say **ax**. (Repeat **ax**.) What's the first sound in **ax**?	(/a/) (short **a**)
Say **ax**. (Repeat **ax**.) Say **ax**. (Repeat **ax**.) What's the last sound in **ax**?	(/s/)
Say **ax**. (Repeat **ax**.) Say **ax**. (Repeat **ax**.) What's the middle sound in **ax**?	(/k/)
Say **quick**. (Repeat **quick**.) Say **quick**. (Repeat **quick**.) What's the second sound in **quick**?	(/w/)
Say **is**. (Repeat **is**.) Say **is**. (Repeat **is**.) What's the last sound in **is**?	(/z/)
Say **zip**. (Repeat **zip**.) Say **zip**. (Repeat **zip**.) What's the middle sound in **zip**?	(/i/) (short **i**)
Say **zip**. (Repeat **zip**.) Say **zip**. (Repeat **zip**.) What's the first sound in **zip**?	(/z/)
Say **fig**. (Repeat **fig**.) Say **fig**. (Repeat **fig**.) What's the last sound in **fig**?	(/g/)
Say **tick**. (Repeat **tick**.) Say **tick**. (Repeat **tick**.) What's the middle sound in **tick**?	(/i/) (short **i**)
Say **quack**. (Repeat **quack**.) Say **quack**. (Repeat **quack**.) What's the first sound in **quack**?	(/k/)
Say **quack**. (Repeat **quack**.) Say **quack**. (Repeat **quack**.) What's the second sound in **quack**?	(/w/)

Stage 3: Phoneme Segmentation and Counting (Spelling the Sounds)

Say **sax**. (Repeat **sax**.) Say **sax**. (Repeat **sax**.) Say the sounds in **sax**.	(/s/ /a/ /k/ /s/)
Say **quick**. (Repeat **quick**.) Say **quick**. (Repeat **quick**.) Say the sounds in **quick**.	(/k/ /w/ /i/ /k/)
Say **yams**. (Repeat **yams**.) Say **yams**. (Repeat **yams**.) Say the sounds in **yams**.	(/y/ /a/ /m/ /s/)
Say **wick**. (Repeat **wick**.) Say **wick**. (Repeat **wick**.) Say the sounds in **wick**.	(/w/ /i/ /k/)
Say **tax**. (Repeat **tax**.) Say **tax**. (Repeat **tax**.) Say the sounds in **tax**.	(/t/ /a/ /k/ /s/)
Say **quiz**. (Repeat **quiz**.) Say **quiz**. (Repeat **quiz**.) Say the sounds in **quiz**.	(/k/ /w/ /i/ /z/)
Say **zip**. (Repeat **zip**.) Say **zip**. (Repeat **zip**.) Say the sounds in **zip**.	(/z/ /i/ /p/)
Say **yam**. (Repeat **yam**.) Say **yam**. (Repeat **yam**.) Say the sounds in **yam**.	(/y/ /a/ /m/)
Say **tick**. (Repeat **tick**.) Say **tick**. (Repeat **tick**.) Say the sounds in **tick**.	(/t/ /i/ /k/)
Say **back**. (Repeat **back**.) Say **back**. (Repeat **back**.) Say the sounds in **back**.	(/b/ /a/ /k/)

After the students have been introduced to the new unit's vocabulary words, you may ask, "How many sounds in **xxx**?" "How many letters in **xxx**?"

Stage 4: Phoneme Blending

Listen and repeat. Listen and repeat: /a/ /k/ /s/. (Repeat phoneme series three times.)   (ax)

Listen and repeat. Listen and repeat: /w/ /i/ /k/. (Repeat phoneme series three times.)   (wick)

Listen and repeat. Listen and repeat: /k/ /w/ /i/ /k/. (Repeat phoneme series three times.)   (quick)

Listen and repeat. Listen and repeat: /m/ /i/ /k/ /s/. (Repeat phoneme series three times.)   (mix)

Listen and repeat. Listen and repeat: /a/ /n/ /d/. (Repeat phoneme series three times.)   (and)

Listen and repeat. Listen and repeat: /w/ /i/ /g/. (Repeat phoneme series three times.)   (wig)

Listen and repeat. Listen and repeat: /y/ /i/ /p/. (Repeat phoneme series three times.)   (yip)

Listen and repeat. Listen and repeat: /s/ /i/ /k/ /s/. (Repeat phoneme series three times.)   (six)

Listen and repeat. Listen and repeat: /t/ /a/ /k/ /s/. (Repeat phoneme series three times.)   (tax)

Stage 5: Rhyming

Say **sax**. (Repeat **sax**.) Say **sax**. (Repeat **sax**.)
Say a word that rhymes with **sax**.   (fax, wax, packs, tacks)

Say **quid**. (Repeat **quid**.) Say **quid**. (Repeat **quid**.)
Say a word that rhymes with **quid**.   (rid, hid, did, lid)

Say **yam**. (Repeat **yam**.) Say **yam**. (Repeat **yam**.)
Say a word that rhymes with **yam**.   (ham, tam, lamb, Pam)

Say **zap**. (Repeat **zap**.) Say **zap**. (Repeat **zap**.)
Say a word that rhymes with **zap**.   (cap, gap, lap, map)

Say **yip**. (Repeat **yip**.) Say **yip**. (Repeat **yip**.)
Say a word that rhymes with **yip**.   (quip, sip, lip, tip)

Say **tack**. (Repeat **tack**.) Say **tack**. (Repeat **tack**.)
Say a word that rhymes with **tack**.   (pack, sack, back, lack)

Say **quiz**. (Repeat **quiz**.) Say **quiz**. (Repeat **quiz**.)
Say a word that rhymes with **quiz**.   (is, his, fizz, Liz)

Stage 6: Phoneme Deletion

Say **quick**. (Repeat **quick**.) Say **quick**. (Repeat **quick**.) Say **quick** without the first /k/.   (/wik/)

Say **mix**. (Repeat **mix**.) Say **mix**. (Repeat **mix**.) Say **mix** without the /s/.   (/mik/)

Say **sick**. (Repeat **sick**.) Say **sick**. (Repeat **sick**.) Say **sick** without the /s/.   (/ik/)

Say **ax**. (Repeat **ax**.) Say **ax**. (Repeat **ax**.) Say **ax** without the /a/.   (/ks/)

Say **yam**. (Repeat **yam**.) Say **yam**. (Repeat **yam**.) Say **yam** without the /y/.   (/am/)

Say **quack**. (Repeat **quack**.) Say **quack**. (Repeat **quack**.) Say **quack** without the /w/.   (/kak/)

Say **yip**. (Repeat **yip**.) Say **yip**. (Repeat **yip**.) Say **yip** without the /y/.   (/ip/)

Say **quill**. (Repeat **quill**.) Say **quill**. (Repeat **quill**.) Say **quill** without the /k/.   (/will/)

Say **zip**. (Repeat **zip**.) Say **zip**. (Repeat **zip**.) Say **zip** without the /p/.   (/zi/)

Say **zag**. (Repeat **zag**.) Say **zag**. (Repeat **zag**.) Say **zag** without the /g/.   (/za/)

Say **zap**. (Repeat **zap**.) Say **zap**. (Repeat **zap**.) Say **zap** without the /z/.   (/ap/)

Say **zig**. (Repeat **zig**.) Say **zig**. (Repeat **zig**.) Say **zig** without the /z/.   (/ig/)

Stage 7: Phoneme Substitution

Say **tip**. (Repeat **tip**.) Say **tip**. (Repeat **tip**.) Now, change the first sound in **tip** to /z/.   (zip)

Say **big**. (Repeat **big**.) Say **big**. (Repeat **big**.) Now, change the first sound in **big** to /w/.   (wig)

Say **back**. (Repeat **back**.) Say **back**. (Repeat **back**.) Now, change the first sound in **back** to /p/.   (pack)

Say **kick**. (Repeat **kick**.) Say **kick**. (Repeat **kick**.) Now, change the first sound in **kick** to /n/.   (Nick)

Say **tin**. (Repeat **tin**.) Say **tin**. (Repeat **tin**.) Now, change the first sound in **tin** to /w/.   (win)

Say **hag**. (Repeat **hag**.) Say **hag**. (Repeat **hag**.) Now, change the first sound in **hag** to /w/.   (wag)

Advancement: After initial phoneme(s), substitute final phoneme(s) and medial phoneme(s):

Say **yak**. (Repeat **yak**.) Say **yak**. (Repeat **tak**.) Now, change the last sound in **yak** to /p/.   (yap)

Say **quill**. (Repeat **quill**.) Say **quill**. (Repeat **quill**.) Now, change the last sound in **quill** to /p/.   (quip)

Say **quit**. (Repeat **quit**.) Say **quit**. (Repeat **quit**.) Now, change the last sound in **quit** to /d/. (quid)

Say **yams**. (Repeat **yams**.) Say **yams**. (Repeat **yams**.) Now, change the first sound in **yams** to /h/.   (hams)

Say **quick**. (Repeat **quick**.) Say **quick**. (Repeat **quick**.) Now, change the middle
sound in **quick** to /a/.   (quack)

Say **quiz**. (Repeat **quiz**.) Say **quiz**. (Repeat **quiz**.) Now, change the last sound in **quiz** to /t/.   (quit)

Say **Max**. (Repeat **Max**.) Say **Max**. (Repeat **Max**.) Now, change the middle sound in **Max** to /i/. (mix)

Say **yap**. (Repeat **yap**.) Say **yap**. (Repeat **yap**.) Now, change the last sound in **yap** to /m/.   (yam)

Say **yap**. (Repeat **yap**.) Say **yap**. (Repeat **yap**.) Now, change the middle sound in **yap** to /i/. (yip)

Say **fix**. (Repeat **fix**.) Say **fix**. (Repeat **fix**.) Now, change the middle sound in **fix** to /a/.   (fax)

Stage 8: Phoneme Reversal

Say **kit**. (Repeat **kit**.) Say **kit**. (Repeat **kit**.)
Now, change the first sound to last, and the last sound to first.   (tick)

Say **pill**. (Repeat **pill**.) Say **pill**. (Repeat **pill**.)
Now, change the first sound to last, and the last sound to first.   (lip)

Say **pack**. (Repeat **pack**.) Say **pack**. (Repeat **pack**.)
Now, change the first sound to last, and the last sound to first.   (cap)

Say **gas**. (Repeat **gas**.) Say **gas**. (Repeat **gas**.)
Now, change the first sound to last, and the last sound to first.   (sag)

Say **zit**. (Repeat **zit**.) Say **zit**. (Repeat **zit**.)
Now, change the first sound to last, and the last sound to first.   ('tis)

Say **pit**. (Repeat **pit**.) Say **pit**. (Repeat **pit**.)
Now, change the first sound to last, and the last sound to first.   (tip)

Say **lap**. (Repeat **lap**.) Say **lap**. (Repeat **lap**.)
Now, change the first sound to last, and the last sound to first.   (pal)

Stage 9: Pig Latin

Three or four modelings may be necessary with this activity, particularly for students with a significant lack of phonemic awareness. Do not penalize students who cannot master Pig Latin.

Say **quick**. (Repeat **quick**.) Say **quick**. (Repeat **quick**.) Say **quick** without the /kw/. (/ik/)

Say /ik/. (Repeat /ik/.) Say /ik/. (Repeat /ik/.) Say /ik/ with /kw/ at the end.   (/ik kw/)

Now, say /ay/ at the end.   (/ik kway/)

Say **zap**. (Repeat **zap**.) Say **zap**. (Repeat **zap**.) Say **zap** without the /z/.   (/ap/)

Say /ap/. (Repeat /ap/.) Say /ap/. (Repeat /ap/.) Say /ap/ with /z/ at the end.   (/ak z/)

Now, say /ay/ at the end.   (/ap zay/)

Say **tax**. (Repeat **tax**.) Say **tax**. (Repeat **tax**.) Say **tax** without the /t/.   (/aks/)

Say /aks/. (Repeat /aks/.) Say /aks/. (Repeat /aks/.) Say /aks/ with /t/ at the end.   (/aks t/)

Now, say /ay/ at the end.   (/aks tay/)

Now, say together in Pig Latin: "I can speak Pig Latin."   (Iay ancay eakspay igpay atinlay)

Spelling Review

The letter **x** represents /*ks*/. The letter **y** represents /*y*/. The letter **z** represents /*z*/. The two letters **qu** represent /*kw*/. The letter **s** represents /*s*/ or /*z*/.

Reading/Spelling Vocabulary

and	mix	Rat Pack	yaps
fix	quick	sax	yips
if	quit	six	zaps
Max	quiz	yams	zig-zag

Unit 8

Phonemic Awareness Drills

These sequential, cumulative drills assess and build phonemic awareness in emerging readers and spellers. To initiate daily lessons, present portions of these drills orally—without corresponding letters. Phonemes (sounds) should be mastered before they are associated with their orthographic representations (letters). After phonemic awareness has been established for a unit's new phonology concepts, students can be introduced to the unit's new symbol-sound correspondences and its reading/spelling vocabulary.

Phonology Concepts for Unit 8

- Consonant sounds (phonemes): Review: /b/, /d/, /f/, /g/, /h/, /j/, /k/, /l/, /m/, /n/, /p/, /r/, /s/, /t/, /v/, /w/, /y/, /z/

- Consonant letters (graphemes): Review: **b**, **c**, **d**, **f**, g, **h**, j, **k**, l, **m**, **n**, **p**, **qu**, **r**, **s**, **t**, **v**, **w**, **x**, **y**, **z**

- Vowel sounds (phonemes):

  – Review: short /a/, short /i/

  – New: short /o/

- Sound-letter (phoneme-grapheme) relationship: /o/ (short **o**) is represented by **o**

Stage 1: Phoneme Production/Replication

Have the students repeat each isolated phoneme:

- Repeat these consonant sounds:

/t/	/s/	/m/	/b/	/k/	/f/	/r/	/h/	/j/	/n/	/l/	/p/	/g/	/d/	/v/	/w/	/qu/	/z/
tan	sat	mat	bat	cat	fat	ran	hat	jab	nab	lap	pat	gap	dad	van	wag	quit	zip

- Repeat these vowel sounds:

/a/	/i/
am	it

- Repeat this new vowel sound:

  /o/
  hot cop pod dock

Stage 2: Phoneme Isolation

Say **bog**. (Repeat **bog**.) Say **bog**. (Repeat **bog**.) What's the first sound in **bog**?   (/b/)

Say **bog**. (Repeat **bog**.) Say **bog**. (Repeat **bog**.) What's the last sound in **bog**?   (/g/)

Say **ox**. (Repeat **ox**.) Say **ox**. (Repeat **ox**.) What's the first sound in **ox**?   (/o/) (short **o**)

Say **ax**. (Repeat **ax**.) Say **ax**. (Repeat **ax**.) What's the first sound in **ax**?   (/a/) (short **a**)

Say **ox**. (Repeat **ox**.) Say **ox**. (Repeat **ox**.) What's the last sound in **ox**?   (/s/)

Say **ox**. (Repeat **ox**.) Say **ox**. (Repeat **ox**.) What's the middle sound in **ox**?   (/k/)

Say **hop**. (Repeat **hop**.) Say **hop**. (Repeat **hop**.) What's the middle sound in **hop**?   (/o/) (short **o**)

Say **hop**. (Repeat **hop**.) Say **hop**. (Repeat **hop**.) What's the middle sound in **hop**?   (/o/) (short **o**)

Say **dock**. (Repeat **dock**.) Say **dock**. (Repeat **dock**.) What's the first sound in **dock**?   (/d/)

Say **Tom**. (Repeat **Tom**.) Say **Tom**. (Repeat **Tom**.) What's the last sound in **Tom**?   (/m/)

Say **fib**. (Repeat **fib**.) Say **fib**. (Repeat **fib**.) What's the middle sound in **fib**?   (/i/) (short **i**)

Say **tax**. (Repeat **tax**.) Say **tax**. (Repeat **tax**.) What's the first sound in **tax**?   (/t/)

Say **doll**. (Repeat **doll**.) Say **doll**. (Repeat **doll**.) What's the last sound in **doll**?   (/l/)

Stage 3: Phoneme Segmentation and Counting (Spelling the Sounds)

Say **socks**. (Repeat **socks**.) Say **socks**. (Repeat **socks**.) Say the sounds in **socks**.   (/s/ /o/ /k/ /s/)

Say **fax**. (Repeat **fax**.) Say **fax**. (Repeat **fax**.) Say the sounds in **fax**.   (/f/ /a/ /k/ /s/)

Say **ox**. (Repeat **ox**.) Say **ox**. (Repeat **ox**.) Say the sounds in **ox**.   (/o/ /k/ /s/)

Say **fix**. (Repeat **fix**.) Say **fix**. (Repeat **fix**.) Say the sounds in **fix**.   (/f/ /i/ /k/ /s/)

Say **lax**. (Repeat **lax**.) Say **lax**. (Repeat **lax**.) Say the sounds in **lax**.   (/l/ /a/ /k/ /s/)

Say **quip**. (Repeat **quip**.) Say **quip**. (Repeat **quip**.) Say the sounds in **quip**.   (/k/ /w/ /i/ /p/)

Say **top**. (Repeat **top**.) Say **top**. (Repeat **top**.) Say the sounds in **top**.   (/t/ /o/ /p/)

Say **pod**. (Repeat **pod**.) Say **pod**. (Repeat **pod**.) Say the sounds in **pod**.   (/p/ /o/ /d/)

Say **box**. (Repeat **box**.) Say **box**. (Repeat **box**.) Say the sounds in **box**.   (/b/ /o/ /k/ /s/)

After the students have been introduced to the new unit's vocabulary words, you may ask, "How many sounds in **xxx**?" "How many letters in **xxx**?"

Stage 4: Phoneme Blending

Listen and repeat. Listen and repeat: /o/ /k/ /s/. (Repeat phoneme series three times.)   (ox)

Listen and repeat. Listen and repeat: /w/ /i/ /k/. (Repeat phoneme series three times.)   (wick)

Listen and repeat. Listen and repeat: /k/ /w/ /i/ /k/. (Repeat phoneme series three times.)   (quick)

Listen and repeat. Listen and repeat: /m/ /i/ /k/ /s/. (Repeat phoneme series three times.)   (mix)

Listen and repeat. Listen and repeat: /a/ /n/ /d/. (Repeat phoneme series three times.)   (and)

Listen and repeat. Listen and repeat: /w/ /i/ /g/. (Repeat phoneme series three times.)   (wig)

Listen and repeat. Listen and repeat: /i/ /z/. (Repeat phoneme series three times.)   (is)

Listen and repeat. Listen and repeat: /s/ /i/ /k/ /s/. (Repeat phoneme series three times.)   (six)

Listen and repeat. Listen and repeat: /t/ /o/ /p/. (Repeat phoneme series three times.)   (top)

Stage 5: Rhyming

Say **fox**. (Repeat **fox**.) Say **fox**. (Repeat **fox**.)
Say a word that rhymes with **fox**.   (box, socks, rocks, lox)

Say **am**. (Repeat **am**.) Say **am**. (Repeat **am**.)
Say a word that rhymes with **am**.   (bam, Sam, ham, Pam)

Say **Rick**. (Repeat **Rick**.) Say **Rick**. (Repeat **Rick**.)
Say a word that rhymes with **Rick**.   (tick, lick, sick, kick)

Say **cob**. (Repeat **cob**.) Say **cob**. (Repeat **cob**.)
Say a word that rhymes with **cob**.   (bob, sob, gob, job)

Say **nod**. (Repeat **nod**.) Say **nod**. (Repeat **nod**.)
Say a word that rhymes with **nod**.   (cod, pod, rod, sod)

Stage 6: Phoneme Deletion

Say **fox**. (Repeat **fox**.) Say **fox**. (Repeat **fox**.) Say **fox** without the /f/.   (/oks/)

Say **pod**. (Repeat **pod**.) Say **pod**. (Repeat **pod**.) Say **pod** without the /p/.   (/od/)

Say **pick**. (Repeat **pick**.) Say **pick**. (Repeat **pick**.) Say **pick** without the /p/.   (/ik/)

Say **fax**. (Repeat **fax**.) Say **fax**. (Repeat **fax**.) Say **fax** without the /f/.   (/aks/)

Say **yam**. (Repeat **yam**.) Say **yam**. (Repeat **yam**.) Say **yam** without the /y/.   (/am/)

Say **din**. (Repeat **din**.) Say **din**. (Repeat **din**.) Say **din** without the /d/.   (/in/)

Say **yip**. (Repeat **yip**.) Say **yip**. (Repeat **yip**.) Say **yip** without the /y/.   (/ip/)

Say **cop**. (Repeat **cop**.) Say **cop**. (Repeat **cop**.) Say **cop** without the /k/.   (/op/)

Say **hop**. (Repeat **hop**.) Say **hop**. (Repeat **hop**.) Say **hop** without the /h/.   (/op/)

Say **zag**. (Repeat **zag**.) Say **zag**. (Repeat **zag**.) Say **zag** without the /g/.   (/za/)

Say **bit**. (Repeat **bit**.) Say **bit**. (Repeat **bit**.) Say **bit** without the /b/.   (/it/)

Say **zig**. (Repeat **zig**.) Say **zig**. (Repeat **zig**.) Say **zig** without the /z/.   (/ig/)

Say **his**. (Repeat **his**.) Say **his**. (Repeat **his**.) Say **his** without the /h/.   (/iz/)

Say **rod**. (Repeat **rod**.) Say **rod**. (Repeat **rod**.) Say **rod** without the /r/.   (/od/)

Stage 7: Phoneme Substitution

Say **fix**. (Repeat **fix**.) Say **fix**. (Repeat **fix**.) Now, change the first sound in **fix** to /m/.   (mix)

Say **zig**. (Repeat **zig**.) Say **zig**. (Repeat **zig**.) Now, change the first sound in **zig** to /w/.   (wig)

Say **sock**. (Repeat **sock**.) Say **sock**. (Repeat **sock**.) Now, change the first sound in **sock** to /d/. (dock)

Say **win**. (Repeat **win**.) Say **win**. (Repeat **win**.) Now, change the first sound in **win** to /t/.   (tin)

Say **hop**. (Repeat **hop**.) Say **hop**. (Repeat **hop**.) Now, change the first sound in **hop** to /t/.   (top)

Say **pot**. (Repeat **pot**.) Say **pot**. (Repeat **pot**.) Now, change the first sound in **pot** to /l/.   (lot)

Advancement: Substitute a mix of initial, final, and medial phoneme(s):

Say **bob**. (Repeat **bob**.) Say **bob**. (Repeat **bob**.) Now, change the first sound in **bob** to /s/. (sob)

Say **mob**. (Repeat **mob**.) Say **mob**. (Repeat **mob**.) Now, change the last sound in **mob** to /p/. (mop)

Say **sock**. (Repeat **sock**.) Say **sock**. (Repeat **sock**.) Now, change the last sound in **sock** to /d/. (sod)

Say **lap**. (Repeat **lap**.) Say **lap**. (Repeat **lap**.) Now, change the first sound in **lap** to /y/. (yap)

Say **rib**. (Repeat **rib**.) Say **rib**. (Repeat **rib**.) Now, change the middle sound in **rib** to /o/. (rob)

Say **quip**. (Repeat **quip**.) Say **quip**. (Repeat **quip**.) Now, change the last sound in **quip** to /z/. (quiz)

Say **jig**. (Repeat **jig**.) Say **jig**. (Repeat **jig**.) Now, change the middle sound in **jig** to /o/. (jog)

Say **cot**. (Repeat **cot**.) Say **cot**. (Repeat **cot**.) Now, change the middle sound in **cot** to /a/. (cat)

Say **tax**. (Repeat **tax**.) Say **tax**. (Repeat **tax**.) Now, change the last sound in **tax** to /t/. (tact)

Say **yap**. (Repeat **yap**.) Say **yap**. (Repeat **yap**.) Now, change the middle sound in **yap** to /i/. (yip)

Say **fix**. (Repeat **fix**.) Say **fix**. (Repeat **fix**.) Now, change the middle sound in **fix** to /a/. (fax)

Stage 8: Phoneme Reversal

Say **pom**. (Repeat **pom**.) Say **pom**. (Repeat **pom**.)
Now, change the first sound to last, and the last sound to first.   (mop)

Say **top**. (Repeat **top**.) Say **top**. (Repeat **top**.)
Now, change the first sound to last, and the last sound to first.   (pot)

Say **got**. (Repeat **got**.) Say **got**. (Repeat **got**.)
Now, change the first sound to last, and the last sound to first.   (tog)

Say **bomb**. (Repeat **bomb**.) Say **bomb**. (Repeat **bomb**.)
Now, change the first sound to last, and the last sound to first.   (mob)

Say **tock**. (Repeat **tock**.) Say **tock**. (Repeat **tock**.)
Now, change the first sound to last, and the last sound to first.   (cot)

Say **dill**. (Repeat **dill**.) Say **dill**. (Repeat **dill**.)
Now, change the first sound to last, and the last sound to first.   (lid)

Say **pass**. (Repeat **pass**.) Say **pass**. (Repeat **pass**.)
Now, change the first sound to last, and the last sound to first.   (sap)

Stage 9: Pig Latin

Three or four modelings may be necessary with this activity, particularly for students with a significant lack of phonemic awareness. Do not penalize students who cannot master Pig Latin.

Say **box**. (Repeat **box**.) Say **box**. (Repeat **box**.) Say **box** without the */b/*.   (/oks/)

Say */oks/*. (Repeat */oks/*.) Say */oks/*. (Repeat */oks/*.) Say */oks/* with */b/* at the end.   (/oks b/)

Now, say */ay/* at the end.   (/oks bay/)

Say **lock**. (Repeat **lock**.) Say **lock**. (Repeat **lock**.) Say **lock** without the */l/*.   (/ok/)

Say */ok/*. (Repeat */ok/*.) Say */ok/*. (Repeat */ok/*.) Say */ok/* with */l/* at the end.   (/ok l/)

Now, say */ay/* at the end.   (/ok lay/)

Say **job**. (Repeat **job**.) Say **job**. (Repeat **job**.) Say **job** without the */j/*.   (/ob/)

Say */ob/*. (Repeat */ob/*.) Say */ob/*. (Repeat */ob/*.) Say */ob/* with */j/* at the end.   (/ob j/)

Now, say */ay/* at the end.   (/ob jay/)

Now, say together in Pig Latin: "I can speak Pig Latin."   (Iay ancay eakspay igpay atinlay)

Reading/Spelling Vocabulary

Bob	dot	Mom	rock	tot
box	hot	nod	sock	*taxi*
cot	job	not	tick-tock	*was*
dock	lock	pop	Tom	
dog	lot	Pop	top	

Unit 9

Phonemic Awareness Drills

These sequential, cumulative drills assess and build phonemic awareness in emerging readers and spellers. To initiate daily lessons, present portions of these drills orally—without corresponding letters. Phonemes (sounds) should be mastered before they are associated with their orthographic representations (letters). After phonemic awareness has been established for a unit's new phonology concepts, students can be introduced to the unit's new symbol-sound correspondences and its reading/spelling vocabulary.

Phonology Concepts for Unit 9

- Consonant sounds (phonemes): Review: /b/, /d/, /f/, /g/, /h/, /j/, /k/, /l/, /m/, /n/, /p/, /r/, /s/, /t/, /v/, /w/, /y/, /z/

- Consonant letters (graphemes): Review: **b**, **c**, **d**, **f**, **g**, **h**, **j**, **k**, **l**, **m**, **n**, **p**, **qu**, **r**, **s**, **t**, **v**, **w**, **x**, **y**, **z**

- Vowel sounds (phonemes): Review: short /a/, short /i/, short /o/

- New: At the end of a word, after a short vowel, the letters **s**, **l**, **f**, and **z** are doubled in spelling: **-ss**, **-ll**, **-ff**, **-zz**

Stage 1: Phoneme Production/Replication

Have the students repeat each isolated phoneme:

- Repeat these consonant sounds:

/t/	/s/	/m/	/b/	/k/	/f/	/r/	/h/	/j/	/n/	/l/	/p/	/g/	/d/	/v/	/w/	/qu/	/z/
tan	sat	mat	bat	cat	fat	ran	hat	jab	nab	lap	pat	gap	dad	van	wag	quit	zip

- Repeat these vowel sounds:

/a/	/i/	/o/
am	it	hot

Stage 2: Phoneme Isolation

Say **sat**. (Repeat **sat**.) Say **sat**. (Repeat **sat**.) What's the first sound in **sat**?　　(/s/)

Say **mass**. (Repeat **mass**.) Say **mass**. (Repeat **mass**.) What's the last sound in **mass**?　(/s/)

Say **lass**. (Repeat **lass**.) Say **lass**. (Repeat **lass**.) What's the first sound in **lass**?　　(/l/)

Say **lip**. (Repeat **lip**.) Say **lip**. (Repeat **lip**.) What's the middle sound in **lip**?　(/i/) (short **i**)

Say **pill**. (Repeat **pill**.) Say **pill**. (Repeat **pill**.) What's the last sound in **pill**?　(/l/)

Say **fizz**. (Repeat **fizz**.) Say **fizz**. (Repeat **fizz**.) What's the middle sound in **fizz**? (/i/) (short **i**)

Say **fob**. (Repeat **fob**.) Say **fob**. (Repeat **fob**.) What's the middle sound in **fob**? (/o/) (short **o**)

Say **jazz**. (Repeat **jazz**.) Say **jazz**. (Repeat **jazz**.) What's the last sound in **jazz**? (/z/)

Say **mop**. (Repeat **mop**.) Say **mop**. (Repeat **mop**.) What's the middle sound in **mop**? (/o/) (short **o**)

Say **fin**. (Repeat **fin**.) Say **fin**. (Repeat **fin**.) What's the first sound in **fin**? (/f/)

Say **pass**. (Repeat **pass**.) Say **pass**. (Repeat **pass**.) What's the last sound in **pass**? (/s/)

Say **fib**. (Repeat **fib**.) Say **fib**. (Repeat **fib**.) What's the middle sound in **fib**? (/i/) (short **i**)

Say **lox**. (Repeat **lox**.) Say **lox**. (Repeat **lox**.) What's the first sound in **lox**? (/l/)

Say **doll**. (Repeat **doll**.) Say **doll**. (Repeat **doll**.) What's the last sound in **doll**? (/l/)

Say **zap**. (Repeat **zap**.) Say **zap**. (Repeat **zap**.) What's the middle sound in **zap**? (/a/) (short **a**)

Stage 3: Phoneme Segmentation and Counting (Spelling the Sounds)

Say **fizz**. (Repeat **fizz**.) Say **fizz**. (Repeat **fizz**.) Say the sounds in **fizz**. (/f/ /i/ /z/)

Say **pass**. (Repeat **pass**.) Say **pass**. (Repeat **pass**.) Say the sounds in **pass**. (/p/ /a/ /s/)

Say **pill**. (Repeat **pill**.) Say **pill**. (Repeat **pill**.) Say the sounds in **pill**. (/p/ /i/ /l/)

Say **kiss**. (Repeat **kiss**.) Say **kiss**. (Repeat **kiss**.) Say the sounds in **kiss**. (/k/ /i/ /s/)

Say **jazz**. (Repeat **jazz**.) Say **jazz**. (Repeat **jazz**.) Say the sounds in **jazz**. (/j/ /a/ /z/)

Say **kill**. (Repeat **kill**.) Say **kill**. (Repeat **kill**.) Say the sounds in **kill**. (/k/ /i/ /l/)

Say **loss**. (Repeat **loss**.) Say **loss**. (Repeat **loss**.) Say the sounds in **loss**. (/l/ /o/ /s/)

Say **quit**. (Repeat **quit**.) Say **quit**. (Repeat **quit**.) Say the sounds in **quit**. (/k/ /w/ /i/ /t/)

Say **his**. (Repeat **his**.) Say **his**. (Repeat **his**.) Say the sounds in **his**. (/h/ /i/ /s/)

After the students have been introduced to the new unit's vocabulary words, you may ask, "How many sounds in **xxx**?" "How many letters in **xxx**?"

Stage 4: Phoneme Blending

Listen and repeat. Listen and repeat: /p/ /a/ /s/. (Repeat phoneme series three times.) (pass)

Listen and repeat. Listen and repeat: /t/ /o/ /s/. (Repeat phoneme series three times.) (toss)

Listen and repeat. Listen and repeat: /k/ /w/ /i/ /k/. (Repeat phoneme series three times.) (quick)

Listen and repeat. Listen and repeat: /j/ /a/ /z/. (Repeat phoneme series three times.) (jazz)

Listen and repeat. Listen and repeat: /b/ /a/ /s/. (Repeat phoneme series three times.) (bass)

Listen and repeat. Listen and repeat: /w/ /i/ /g/. (Repeat phoneme series three times.)   (wig)

Listen and repeat. Listen and repeat: /d/ /o/ /l/. (Repeat phoneme series three times.)   (doll)

Listen and repeat. Listen and repeat: /k/ /w/ /i/ /l/. (Repeat phoneme series three times.)   (quill)

Listen and repeat. Listen and repeat: /d/ /o/ /f/. (Repeat phoneme series three times.)   (doff)

Stage 5: Rhyming

Say **pill**. (Repeat **pill**.) Say **pill**. (Repeat **pill**.)
Say a word that rhymes with **pill**.   (ill, sill, bill)

Say **mass**. (Repeat **mass**.) Say **mass**. (Repeat **mass**.)
Say a word that rhymes with **mass**.   (sass, pass, lass)

Say **moss**. (Repeat **moss**.) Say **moss**. (Repeat **moss**.)
Say a word that rhymes with **moss**.   (boss, loss, toss)

Say **hop**. (Repeat **hop**.) Say **hop**. (Repeat **hop**.)
Say a word that rhymes with **hop**.   (top, cop, pop)

Stage 6: Phoneme Deletion

Say **lob**. (Repeat **lob**.) Say **lob**. (Repeat **lob**.) Say **lob** without the /l/.   (/ob/)

Say **ram**. (Repeat **ram**.) Say **ram**. (Repeat **ram**.) Say **ram** without the /r/.   (/am/)

Say **pill**. (Repeat **pill**.) Say **pill**. (Repeat **pill**.) Say **pill** without the /p/.   (/il/)

Say **hid**. (Repeat **hid**.) Say **hid**. (Repeat **hid**.) Say **hid** without the /h/.   (/id/)

Say **quill**. (Repeat **quill**.) Say **quill**. (Repeat **quill**.) Say **quill** without the /k/.   (/wil/)

Say **pod**. (Repeat **pod**.) Say **pod**. (Repeat **pod**.) Say **pod** without the /p/.   (/od/)

Say **win**. (Repeat **win**.) Say **win**. (Repeat **win**.) Say **win** without the /w/.   (/in/)

Say **rock**. (Repeat **rock**.) Say **rock**. (Repeat **rock**.) Say **rock** without the /k/.   (/ro/)

Say **jazz**. (Repeat **jazz**.) Say **jazz**. (Repeat **jazz**.) Say **jazz** without the /j/.   (/az/)

Say **pit**. (Repeat **pit**.) Say **pit**. (Repeat **pit**.) Say **pit** without the /p/.   (/it/)

Say **fizz**. (Repeat **fizz**.) Say **fizz**. (Repeat **fizz**.) Say **fizz** without the /f/.   (/iz/)

Say **pat**. (Repeat **pat**.) Say **pat**. (Repeat **pat**.) Say **pat** without the /p/.   (/at/)

Say **hiss**. (Repeat **hiss**.) Say **hiss**. (Repeat **hiss**.) Say **hiss** without the /h/.   (/is/)

Say **pot**. (Repeat **pot**.) Say **pot**. (Repeat **pot**.) Say **pot** without the /p/.   (/ot/)

Stage 7: Phoneme Substitution

Say **sill**. (Repeat **sill**.) Say **sill**. (Repeat **sill**.) Now, change the first sound in **sill** to /p/.   (pill)

Say **tin**. (Repeat **tin**.) Say **tin**. (Repeat **tin**.) Now, change the first sound in **tin** to /w/.   (win)

Say **yak**. (Repeat **yak**.) Say **yak**. (Repeat **yak**.) Now, change the first sound in **yak** to /s/.   (sack)

Say **sit**. (Repeat **sit**.) Say **sit**. (Repeat **sit**.) Now, change the first sound in **sit** to /p/.   (pit)

Say **toss**. (Repeat **toss**.) Say **toss**. (Repeat **toss**.) Now, change the first sound in **toss** to /l/.   (loss)

Say **pass**. (Repeat **pass**.) Say **pass**. (Repeat **pass**.) Now, change the first sound in **pass** to /b/.   (bass)

Advancement: Substitute a mix of initial, final, and medial phoneme(s):

Say **job**. (Repeat **job**.) Say **job**. (Repeat **job**.) Now, change the first sound in **job** to /s/.   (sob)

Say **mop**. (Repeat **mop**.) Say **mop**. (Repeat **mop**.) Now, change the last sound in **mop** to /k/. (mock)

Say **sock**. (Repeat **sock**.) Say **sock**. (Repeat **sock**.) Now, change the last sound in **sock** to /d/. (sod)

Say **gap**. (Repeat **gap**.) Say **gap**. (Repeat **gap**.) Now, change the first sound in **gap** to /y/.   (yap)

Say **rib**. (Repeat **rib**.) Say **rib**. (Repeat **rib**.) Now, change the middle sound in **rib** to /o/.   (rob)

Say **hit**. (Repeat **hit**.) Say **hit**. (Repeat **hit**.) Now, change the last sound in **hit** to /z/.   (his)

Say **jig**. (Repeat **jig**.) Say **jig**. (Repeat **jig**.) Now, change the middle sound in **jig** to /o/.   (jog)

Say **bat**. (Repeat **bat**.) Say **bat**. (Repeat **bat**.) Now, change the middle sound in **bat** to /i/.   (bit)

Say **pill**. (Repeat **pill**.) Say **pill**. (Repeat **pill**.) Now, change the last sound in **pill** to /t/.   (pit)

Say **yap**. (Repeat **yap**.) Say **yap**. (Repeat **yap**.) Now, change the middle sound in **yap** to /i/.   (yip)

Say **pat**. (Repeat **pat**.) Say **pat**. (Repeat **pat**.) Now, change the middle sound in **pat** to /o/.   (pot)

Stage 8: Phoneme Reversal

Say **pill**. (Repeat **pill**.) Say **pill**. (Repeat **pill**.)
Now, change the first sound to last, and the last sound to first.   (lip)

Say **dock**. (Repeat **dock**.) Say **dock**. (Repeat **dock**.)
Now, change the first sound to last, and the last sound to first.   (cod)

Say **kiss**. (Repeat **kiss**.) Say **kiss**. (Repeat **kiss**.)
Now, change the first sound to last, and the last sound to first.   (sick)

Say **dill**. (Repeat **dill**.) Say **dill**. (Repeat **dill**.)
Now, change the first sound to last, and the last sound to first.   (lid)

Say **sag**. (Repeat **sag**.) Say **sag**. (Repeat **sag**.)
Now, change the first sound to last, and the last sound to first.   (gas)

Say **top**. (Repeat **top**.) Say **top**. (Repeat **top**.)
Now, change the first sound to last, and the last sound to first.   (pot)

Say **got**. (Repeat **got**.) Say **got**. (Repeat **got**.)
Now, change the first sound to last, and the last sound to first.   (tog)

Stage 9: Pig Latin

Three or four modelings may be necessary with this activity, particularly for students with a significant lack of phonemic awareness. Do not penalize students who cannot master Pig Latin.

Say **jazz**. (Repeat **jazz**.) Say **jazz**. (Repeat **jazz**.) Say **jazz** without the */j/*.   (*/az/*)

Say */az/*. (Repeat */az/*.) Say */az/*. (Repeat */az/*.) Say */az/* with */j/* at the end.   (*/az j/*)

Now, say */ay/* at the end.   (*/az jay/*)

Say **miss**. (Repeat **miss**.) Say **miss**. (Repeat **miss**.) Say **miss** without the */m/*.   (*/is/*)

Say */is/*. (Repeat */is/*.) Say */is/*. (Repeat */is/*.) Say */is/* with */m/* at the end.   (*/is m/*)

Now, say */ay/* at the end.   (*/is may/*)

Say **doff**.* (Repeat **doff**.) Say **doff**. (Repeat **doff**.) Say **doff** without the */d/*.   (*/of/*)

Say */of/*. (Repeat */of/*.) Say */of/*. (Repeat */of/*.) Say */of/* with */d/* at the end.   (*/of d/*)

Now, say */ay/* at the end.   (*/of day/*)

Now, say together in Pig Latin: "I can speak Pig Latin."   (Iay ancay eakspay igpay atinlay)

* Just for fun: The words **doff** and **don** came from Old English: "do off" and "do on."

Spelling Review

At the end of a word, after a short vowel, the letters **-s**, **-l**, **-f**, and **-z** are doubled: **-ss**, **-ll**, **-ff**, **-zz**.

Reading/Spelling Vocabulary

Bill	jazz	Liz	pill	till
doll	Jill	Miss	Pitt	toss
hill	kiss	off	quill	will
hiss	lass	pass	sill	*you*

Unit 10

Phonemic Awareness Drills

These sequential, cumulative drills assess and build phonemic awareness in emerging readers and spellers. To initiate daily lessons, present portions of these drills orally—without corresponding letters. Phonemes (sounds) should be mastered before they are associated with their orthographic representations (letters). After phonemic awareness has been established for a unit's new phonology concepts, students can be introduced to the unit's new symbol-sound correspondences and its reading/spelling vocabulary.

Phonology Concepts for Unit 10

- Consonant sounds (phonemes): Review: /b/, /d/, /f/, /g/, /h/, /j/, /k/, /l/, /m/, /n/, /p/, /r/, /s/, /t/, /v/, /w/, /y/, /z/

- Consonant letters (graphemes): Review: **b**, **c**, **d**, **f**, **g**, **h**, **j**, **k**, **l**, **m**, **n**, **p**, **qu**, **r**, **s**, **t**, **v**, **w**, **x**, **y**, **z**

- Vowel sounds (phonemes): Review: short /a/, short /i/, short /o/

- New: At the ends of words, the consonant sounds /n/ and /g/ unite to form /ŋ/: **-ng** represents /ŋ/; **-nk** represents /ŋk/. For readers and spellers, **-ng**, will count as one phoneme and two graphemes; **-nk** will count as two phonemes and two graphemes.

Stage 1: Phoneme Production/Replication

Have the students repeat each isolated phoneme:

- Repeat these consonant sounds:

/t/	/s/	/m/	/b/	/k/	/f/	/r/	/h/	/j/	/n/	/l/	/p/	/g/	/d/	/v/	/w/	/qu/	/z/
tan	sat	mat	bat	cat	fat	ran	hat	jab	nab	lap	pat	gap	dad	van	wag	quit	zip

- Repeat these vowel sounds:

/a/	/i/	/o/
am	it	hot

- Repeat these new consonant sound combinations:

/ŋ/	/ŋk/
bang	honk

(Instructor: Hereafter, /ng/: **-ng** will be used for /ŋ/; /nk/: **-nk** will be used for /ŋk/.)

Stage 2: Phoneme Isolation

Say **bank**. (Repeat **bank**.) Say **bank**. (Repeat **bank**.) Say the last two sounds in **bank**.   (/nk/)

Say **quip**. (Repeat **quip**.) Say **quip**. (Repeat **quip**.) Say the first two sounds in **quip**.   (/kw/)

Say **ax**. (Repeat **ax**.) Say **ax**. (Repeat **ax**.) Say the last two sounds in **ax**.   (/ks/)

Say **rink**. (Repeat **rink**.) Say **rink**. (Repeat **rink**.) Say the first two sounds in **rink**.   (/ri/)

Say **tong**. (Repeat **tong**.) Say **tong**. (Repeat **tong**.) Say the last sound in **tong**.   (/ng/)

Say **sank**. (Repeat **sank**.) Say **sank**. (Repeat **sank**.) Say the first two sounds in **sank**.   (/sa/)

Say **sank**. (Repeat **sank**.) Say **sank**. (Repeat **sank**.) Say the last two sounds in **sank**.   (/nk/)

Say **sing**. (Repeat **sing**.) Say **sing**. (Repeat **sing**.) Say the first two sounds in **sing**.   (/si/)

Say **sing**. (Repeat **sing**.) Say **sing**. (Repeat **sing**.) Say the last sound in **sing**.   (/ng/)

Say **bang**. (Repeat **bang**.) Say **bang**. (Repeat **bang**.) Say the first two sounds in **bang**.   (/ba/)

Say **bang**. (Repeat **bang**.) Say **bang**. (Repeat **bang**.) Say the last sound in **bang**.   (/ng/)

Say **wink**. (Repeat **wink**.) Say **wink**. (Repeat **wink**.) Say the first two sounds in **wink**.   (/wi/)

Say **wink**. (Repeat **wink**.) Say **wink**. (Repeat **wink**.) Say the last two sounds in **wink**.   (/nk/)

Stage 3: Phoneme Segmentation and Counting (Spelling the Sounds)

Say **rank**. (Repeat **rank**.) Say **rank**. (Repeat **rank**.) Say the sounds in **rank**.   (/r/ /a/ /ng/ /k/)

Say **sill**. (Repeat **sill**.) Say **sill**. (Repeat **sill**.) Say the sounds in **sill**.   (/s/ /i/ /l/)

Say **sing**. (Repeat **sing**.) Say **sing**. (Repeat **sing**.) Say the sounds in **sing**.   (/s/ /i/ /ng/)

Say **fizz**. (Repeat **fizz**.) Say **fizz**. (Repeat **fizz**.) Say the sounds in **fizz**.   (/f/ /i/ /z/)

Say **jazz**. (Repeat **jazz**.) Say **jazz**. (Repeat **jazz**.) Say the sounds in **jazz**.   (/j/ /a/ /z/)

Say **pill**. (Repeat **pill**.) Say **pill**. (Repeat **pill**.) Say the sounds in **pill**.   (/p/ /i/ /l/)

Say **pass**. (Repeat **pass**.) Say **pass**. (Repeat **pass**.) Say the sounds in **pass**.   (/p/ /a/ /s/)

Say **wing**. (Repeat **wing**.) Say **wing**. (Repeat **wing**.) Say the sounds in **wing**.   (/w/ /i/ /ng/)

Say **bank**. (Repeat **bank**.) Say **bank**. (Repeat **bank**.) Say the sounds in **bank**.   (/b/ /a/ /ng/ /k/)

After the students have been introduced to the new unit's vocabulary words, you may ask, "How many sounds in **xxx**?" "How many letters in **xxx**?"

Stage 4: Phoneme Blending

Listen and repeat. Listen and repeat: /o/ /k/ /s/. (Repeat phoneme series three times.)   (ox)

Listen and repeat. Listen and repeat: /w/ /i/ /ng/ /k/. (Repeat phoneme series three times.)   (wink)

Listen and repeat. Listen and repeat: /k/ /w/ /i/ /k/. (Repeat phoneme series three times.)   (quick)

Listen and repeat. Listen and repeat: /m/ /i/ /k/ /s/. (Repeat phoneme series three times.)   (mix)

Listen and repeat. Listen and repeat: /s/ /o/ /ng/. (Repeat phoneme series three times.)   (song)

Listen and repeat. Listen and repeat: /b/ /a/ /ng/ /k/. (Repeat phoneme series three times.)   (bank)

Listen and repeat. Listen and repeat: /s/ /i/ /ng/ /k/. (Repeat phoneme series three times.)   (sink)

Listen and repeat. Listen and repeat: /d/ /i/ /ng/. (Repeat phoneme series three times.)   (ding)

Listen and repeat. Listen and repeat: /g/ /a/ /ng/. (Repeat phoneme series three times.)   (gang)

Stage 5: Rhyming

Say **bank**. (Repeat **bank**.) Say **bank**. (Repeat **bank**.)
Say a word that rhymes with **bank**.   (dank, lank, rank, sank)

Say **sing**. (Repeat **sing**.) Say **sing**. (Repeat **sing**.)
Say a word that rhymes with **sing**.   (ring, bing, ding, king)

Say **pill**. (Repeat **pill**.) Say **pill**. (Repeat **pill**.)
Say a word that rhymes with **pill**.   (sill, quill, bill, dill)

Say **rink**. (Repeat **rink**.) Say **rink**. (Repeat **rink**.)
Say a word that rhymes with **rink**.   (link, mink, pink, sink)

Stage 6: Phoneme Deletion

Say **sink**. (Repeat **sink**.) Say **sink**. (Repeat **sink**.) Say **sink** without the /s/.   (/ink/)

Say **fox**. (Repeat **fox**.) Say **fox**. (Repeat **fox**.) Say **fox** without the /f/.   (/oks/)

Say **pill**. (Repeat **pill**.) Say **pill**. (Repeat **pill**.) Say **pill** without the /p/.   (/ill/)

Say **ring**. (Repeat **ring**.) Say **ring**. (Repeat **ring**.) Say **ring** without the /r/.   (/ing/)

Say **jazz**. (Repeat **jazz**.) Say **jazz**. (Repeat **jazz**.) Say **jazz** without the /j/.   (/azz/)

Say **rank**. (Repeat **rank**.) Say **rank**. (Repeat **rank**.) Say **rank** without the /r/.   (/ank/)

Say **yam**. (Repeat **yam**.) Say **yam**. (Repeat **yam**.) Say **yam** without the /y/.   (/am/)

Say **wink**. (Repeat **wink**.) Say **wink**. (Repeat **wink**.) Say **wink** without the /nk/.   (/wi/)

Say **ring**. (Repeat **ring**.) Say **ring**. (Repeat **ring**.) Say **ring** without the /r/.   (/ing/)

Say **rank**. (Repeat **rank**.) Say **rank**. (Repeat **rank**.) Say **rank** without the /nk/.   (/ra/)

Say **bang**. (Repeat **bang**.) Say **bang**. (Repeat **bang**.) Say **bang** without the /b/.   (/ang/)

Say **bang**. (Repeat **bang**.) Say **bang**. (Repeat **bang**.) Say **bang** without the /ng/.   (/ba/)

Say **bank**. (Repeat **bank**.) Say **bank**. (Repeat **bank**.) Say **bank** without the /b/.   (/ank/)

Say **sing**. (Repeat **sing**.) Say **sing**. (Repeat **sing**.) Say **sing** without the /ng/.   (/si/)

Stage 7: Phoneme Substitution

Say **rank**. (Repeat **rank**.) Say **rank**. (Repeat **rank**.) Now, change the first sound in **rank** to /b/.   (bank)

Say **link**. (Repeat **link**.) Say **link**. (Repeat **link**.) Now, change the first sound in **link** to /w/.   (wink)

Say **tong**. (Repeat **tong**.) Say **tong**. (Repeat **tong**.) Now, change the first sound in **tong** to /l/. (long)

Say **honk**. (Repeat **honk**.) Say **honk**. (Repeat **honk**.) Now, change the first sound in **honk** to /b/.   (bonk)

Say **sing**. (Repeat **sing**.) Say **sing**. (Repeat **sing**.) Now, change the first sound in **sing** to /k/.   (king)

Say **rink**. (Repeat **rink**.) Say **rink**. (Repeat **rink**.) Now, change the first sound in **rink** to /l/.   (link)

Advancement: Substitute initial, final, and medial phoneme(s):

Say **link**. (Repeat **link**.) Say **link**. (Repeat **link**.) Now, change the first sound in **link** to /s/. (sink)

Say **bank**. (Repeat **bank**.) Say **bank**. (Repeat **bank**.) Now, change the last sound in **bank** to /g/. (bang)

Say **sing**. (Repeat **sing**.) Say **sing**. (Repeat **sing**.) Now, change the first sound in **sing** to /w/.   (wing)

Say **hang**. (Repeat **hang**.) Say **hang**. (Repeat **hang**.) Now, change the first sound in **hang** to /f/. (fang)

Say **sink**. (Repeat **sink**.) Say **sink**. (Repeat **sink**.) Now, change the middle sound in **sink** to /a/. (sank)

Say **jam**. (Repeat **jam**.) Say **jam**. (Repeat **jam**.) Now, change the last sound in **jam** to /z/.   (jazz)

Say **jig**. (Repeat **jig**.) Say **jig**. (Repeat **jig**.) Now, change the middle sound in **jig** to /o/.   (jog)

Say **rot**. (Repeat **rot**.) Say **rot**. (Repeat **rot**.) Now, change the middle sound in **rot** to /a/.   (rat)

Say **cob**. (Repeat **cob**.) Say **cob**. (Repeat **cob**.) Now, change the last sound in **cob** to /t/.   (cot)

Say **bet**. (Repeat **bet**.) Say **bet**. (Repeat **bet**.) Now, change the middle sound in **bet** to /i/.   (bit)

Say **rig**. (Repeat **rig**.) Say **rig**. (Repeat **rig**.) Now, change the middle sound in **rig** to /a/.   (rag)

Stage 8: Phoneme Reversal

Say **tip**. (Repeat **tip**.) Say **tip**. (Repeat **tip**.)
Now, change the first sound to last, and the last sound to first.   (pit)

Say **pot**. (Repeat **pot**.) Say **pot**. (Repeat **pot**.)
Now, change the first sound to last, and the last sound to first.   (top)

Say **got**. (Repeat **got**.) Say **got**. (Repeat **got**.)
Now, change the first sound to last, and the last sound to first.   (tog)

Say **bomb**. (Repeat **bomb**.) Say **bomb**. (Repeat **bomb**.)
Now, change the first sound to last, and the last sound to first.   (mob)

Say **tock**. (Repeat **tock**.) Say **tock**. (Repeat **tock**.)
Now, change the first sound to last, and the last sound to first.   (cot)

Say **dill**. (Repeat **dill**.) Say **dill**. (Repeat **dill**.)
Now, change the first sound to last, and the last sound to first.   (lid)

Say **pass**. (Repeat **pass**.) Say **pass**. (Repeat **pass**.)
Now, change the first sound to last, and the last sound to first.   (sap)

Stage 9: Pig Latin

Three or four modelings may be necessary with this activity, particularly for students with a significant lack of phonemic awareness. Do not penalize students who cannot master Pig Latin.

Say **bang**. (Repeat **bang**.) Say **bang**. (Repeat **bang**.) Say **bang** without the /b/.   (/ang/)

Say /ang/. (Repeat /ang/.) Say /ang/. (Repeat /ang/.) Say /ang/ with /b/ at the end.   (/ang b/)

Now, say /ay/ at the end.   (/ang bay/)

Say **link**. (Repeat **link**.) Say **link**. (Repeat **link**.) Say **link** without the /l/.   (/ink/)

Say /ink/. (Repeat /ink/.) Say /ink/. (Repeat /ink/.) Say /ink/ with /l/ at the end.   (/ink l/)

Now, say /ay/ at the end.   (/ink lay/)

Say **wing**. (Repeat **wing**.) Say **wing**. (Repeat **wing**.) Say **wing** without the /w/.   (/ing/)

Say /ing/. (Repeat /ing/.) Say /ing/. (Repeat /ing/.) Say /ing/ with /w/ at the end.   (/ing w/)

Now, say /ay/ at the end.   (/ing way/)

Now, say together in Pig Latin: "I can speak Pig Latin."   (Iay ancay eakspay igpay atinlay)

Spelling Review

At the end of a word, after a short vowel, the letters **-s**, **-l**, **-f**, and **-z** are doubled: **-ss**, **-ll**, **-ff**, **-zz**.

Reading/Spelling Vocabulary

bang	honk	rank	sing	yank
ding-dong	king	ring	sink	*what*
gang	long	rink	song	
gong	pink	sang	wings	

Unit 11

Phonemic Awareness Drills

These sequential, cumulative drills assess and build phonemic awareness in emerging readers and spellers. To initiate daily lessons, present portions of these drills orally—without corresponding letters. Phonemes (sounds) should be mastered before they are associated with their orthographic representations (letters). After phonemic awareness has been established for a unit's new phonology concepts, students can be introduced to the unit's new symbol-sound correspondences and its reading/spelling vocabulary.

Phonology Concepts for Unit 11

- Consonant sounds (phonemes): Review: /b/, /d/, /f/, /g/, /h/, /j/, /k/, /l/, /m/, /n/, /p/, /r/, /s/, /t/, /v/, /w/, /y/, /z/

- Consonant letters (graphemes): Review: <u>**b**</u>, <u>**c**</u>, <u>**d**</u>, **f**, **g**, <u>**h**</u>, **j**, <u>**k**</u>, <u>**l**</u>, <u>**m**</u>, **n**, **p**, <u>**qu**</u>, <u>**r**</u>, <u>**s**</u>, <u>**t**</u>, <u>**v**</u>, <u>**w**</u>, <u>**x**</u>, **y**, **z**

- Vowel sounds (phonemes): Review: short /a/, short /i/, short /o/

- New: Consonant digraphs: two consonant letters (graphemes) used to represent one consonant sound (phoneme) that is different from either letter's usual sound: <u>**wh**</u>, <u>**ch**</u>, <u>**th**</u>, <u>**sh**</u>

Stage 1: Phoneme Production/Replication

Have the students repeat each of these new sounds:

/th/　/t<u>h</u>/,　/ch/　/sh/,　/wh/　/w/
thin　them　chip　ship　whim　win

Instructor: Demonstrate the difference between voiced /t<u>h</u>/ (as in them) and voiceless /th/ (as in thin).

Stage 2: Phoneme Isolation

Say **chuck**. (Repeat **chuck**.) Say **chuck**. (Repeat **chuck**.)
What's the first sound in **chuck**?　　　　　　　　　　　　　　　(/ch/)

Say **math**. (Repeat **math**.) Say **math**. (Repeat **math**.)
What's the last sound in **math**?　　　　　　　　　　　　　　　(/th/)

Say **which**. (Repeat **which**.) Say **which**. (Repeat **which**.)
What's the middle sound in **which**?　　　　　　　　　　　　　(/i/) (short **i**)

Say **shed**. (Repeat **shed**.) Say **shed**. (Repeat **shed**.)
What's the first sound in **shed**?　　　　　　　　　　　　　　(/sh/)

Say **bath**. (Repeat **bath**.) Say **bath**. (Repeat **bath**.)
What's the last sound in **bath**?   (/*th*/)

Say **chop**. (Repeat **chop**.) Say **chop**. (Repeat **chop**.)
What's the middle sound in **chop**?   (/*o*/) (short **o**)

Say **which**. (Repeat **which**.) Say **which**. (Repeat **which**.)
What's the first sound in **which**?   (/*wh*/)

Say **wish**. (Repeat **wish**.) Say **wish**. (Repeat **wish**.)
What's the last sound in **wish**?   (/*sh*/)

Say **mash**. (Repeat **mash**.) Say **mash**. (Repeat **mash**.)
What's the middle sound in **mash**?   (/*a*/) (short **a**)

Say **this**. (Repeat **this**.) Say **this**. (Repeat **this**.)
What's the first sound in **this**?   (/*th*/)

Say **chop**. (Repeat **chop**.) Say **chop**. (Repeat **chop**.)
What's the middle sound in **chop**?   (/*o*/) (short **o**)

Say **rich**. (Repeat **rich**.) Say **rich**. (Repeat **rich**.)
What's the last sound in **rich**?   (/*ch*/)

Say **when**. (Repeat **when**.) Say **when**. (Repeat **when**.)
What's the first sound in **when**?   (/*wh*/)

Stage 3: Phoneme Segmentation and Counting (Spelling the Sounds)

Say **which**. (Repeat **which**.) Say **which**. (Repeat **which**.) Say the sounds in **which**.   (/*wh*/ /*i*/ /*ch*/)

Say **than**. (Repeat **than**.) Say **than**. (Repeat **than**.) Say the sounds in **than**.   (/*th*/ /*a*/ /*n*/)

Say **chill**. (Repeat **chill**.) Say **chill**. (Repeat **chill**.) Say the sounds in **chill**.   (/*ch*/ /*i*/ /*l*/)

Say **chick**. (Repeat **chick**.) Say **chick**. (Repeat **chick**.) Say the sounds in **chick**.   (/*ch*/ /*i*/ /*k*/)

Say **whiff**. (Repeat **whiff**.) Say **whiff**. (Repeat **whiff**.) Say the sounds in **whiff**.   (/*wh*/ /*i*/ /*f*/)

Say **shop**. (Repeat **shop**.) Say **shop**. (Repeat **shop**.) Say the sounds in **shop**.   (/*sh*/ /*o*/ /*p*/)

Say **ax**. (Repeat **ax**.) Say **ax**. (Repeat **ax**.) Say the sounds in **ax**.   (/*a*/ /*k*/ /*s*/)

Say **whip**. (Repeat **whip**.) Say **whip**. (Repeat **whip**.) Say the sounds in **whip**.   (/*wh*/ /*i*/ /*p*/)

Say **thing**. (Repeat **thing**.) Say **thing**. (Repeat **thing**.) Say the sounds in **thing**.   (/*th*/ /*i*/ /*n*/ /*g*/)

Say **thank**. (Repeat **thank**.) Say **thank**. (Repeat **thank**.) Say the sounds in **thank**.   (/*th*/ /*a*/ /*n*/ /*k*/)

After the students have been introduced to the new unit's vocabulary words, you may ask, "How many sounds in **xxx**?" "How many letters in **xxx**?"

Stage 4: Phoneme Blending

Listen and repeat. Listen and repeat: /sh/ /o/ /t/. (Repeat phoneme series three times.)   (shot)

Listen and repeat. Listen and repeat: /m/ /a/ /th/. (Repeat phoneme series three times.)   (math)

Listen and repeat. Listen and repeat: /wh/ /i/ /ch/. (Repeat phoneme series three times.)   (which)

Listen and repeat. Listen and repeat: /s/ /a/ /sh/. (Repeat phoneme series three times.)   (sash)

Listen and repeat. Listen and repeat: /th/ /i/ /s/. (Repeat phoneme series three times.)   (this)

Listen and repeat. Listen and repeat: /wh/ /a/ /m/. (Repeat phoneme series three times.)   (wham)

Stage 5: Rhyming

Say **math**. (Repeat **math**.) Say **math**. (Repeat **math**.)
Say a word that rhymes with **math**.   (bath, path, wrath)

Say **cash**. (Repeat **cash**.) Say **cash**. (Repeat **cash**.)
Say a word that rhymes with **cash**.   (dash, hash, mash)

Say **whip**. (Repeat **whip**.) Say **whip**. (Repeat **whip**.)
Say a word that rhymes with **whip**.   (dip, lip, nip)

Say **than**. (Repeat **than**.) Say **than**. (Repeat **than**.)
Say a word that rhymes with **than**.   (can, ban, fan)

Say **shop**. (Repeat **shop**.) Say **shop**. (Repeat **shop**.)
Say a word that rhymes with **shop**.   (hop, drop, mop)

Say **when**. (Repeat **when**.) Say **when**. (Repeat **when**.)
Say a word that rhymes with **when**.   (men, wren, pen)

Say **chick**. (Repeat **chick**.) Say **chick**. (Repeat **chick**.)
Say a word that rhymes with **chick**.   (sick, lick, pick)

Say **thin**. (Repeat **thin**.) Say **thin**. (Repeat **thin**.)
Say a word that rhymes with **thin**.   (bin, shin, chin)

Stage 6: Phoneme Deletion

Say **chin**. (Repeat **chin**.) Say **chin**. (Repeat **chin**.) Say **chin** without the /ch/.   (/in/)

Say **sham**. (Repeat **sham**.) Say **sham**. (Repeat **sham**.) Say **sham** without the /sh/.   (/am/)

Say **whiff**. (Repeat **whiff**.) Say **whiff**. (Repeat **whiff**.) Say **whiff** without the /wh/.   (/if/)

Say **this**. (Repeat **this**.) Say **this**. (Repeat **this**.) Say **this** without the /s/.   (/thi/)

Say **which**. (Repeat **which**.) Say **which**. (Repeat **which**.) Say **which** without the /wh/.   (/ich/)

Say **wish**. (Repeat **wish**.) Say **wish**. (Repeat **wish**.) Say **wish** without the /w/.   (/ish/)

Say **bath**. (Repeat **bath**.) Say **bath**. (Repeat **bath**.) Say **bath** without the /th/.   (/ba/)

Say **tang**. (Repeat **tang**.) Say **tang**. (Repeat **tang**.) Say **tang** without the /t/.   (/ang/)

Say **posh**. (Repeat **posh**.) Say **posh**. (Repeat **posh**.) Say **posh** without the /p/.   (/osh/)

Say **sink**. (Repeat **sink**.) Say **sink**. (Repeat **sink**.) Say **sink** without the /s/.   (/ink/)

Say **thick**. (Repeat **thick**.) Say **thick**. (Repeat **thick**.) Say **thick** without the /th/.   (/ik/)

Say **chat**. (Repeat **chat**.) Say **chat**. (Repeat **chat**.) Say **chat** without the /ch/.   (/at/)

Stage 7: Phoneme Substitution

Say **chip**. (Repeat **chip**.) Say **chip**. (Repeat **chip**.) Now, change the first sound in **chip** to /sh/.

(ship)

Say **math**. (Repeat **math**.) Say **math**. (Repeat **math**.) Now, change the first sound in **math** to /b/.

(bath)

Say **thick**. (Repeat **thick**.) Say **thick**. (Repeat **thick**.) Now, change the first sound in **thick** to /ch/.

(chick)

Say **whip**. (Repeat **whip**.) Say **whip**. (Repeat **whip**.) Now, change the first sound in **whip** to /sh/.

(ship)

Say **shop**. (Repeat **shop**.) Say **shop**. (Repeat **shop**.) Now, change the first sound in **shop** to /ch/.

(chop)

Say **whack**. (Repeat **whack**.) Say **whack**. (Repeat **whack**.) Now, change the first sound in **whack** to /sh/.

(shack)

Advancement: After initial phoneme(s), substitute final phoneme(s) and medial phoneme(s):

Say **thin**. (Repeat **thin**.) Say **thin**. (Repeat **thin**.) Now, change the last sound in **thin** to /k/.

(thick)

Say **shack**. (Repeat **shack**.) Say **shack**. (Repeat **shack**.) Now, change the middle sound in **shack** to /o/.

(shock)

Say **whack**. (Repeat **whack**.) Say **whack**. (Repeat **whack**.) Now, change the last sound in **whack** to /m/.

(wham)

Say **dash**. (Repeat **dash**.) Say **dash**. (Repeat **dash**.) Now, change the middle sound in **dash** to /i/.

(dish)

Say **chick**. (Repeat **chick**.) Say **chick**. (Repeat **chick**.) Now, change the last sound in **chick** to /n/.

(chin)

Say **whip**. (Repeat **whip**.) Say **whip**. (Repeat **whip**.) Now, change the middle sound in **whip** to /a/.

(whap)

Say **ship**. (Repeat **ship**.) Say **ship**. (Repeat **ship**.) Now, change the first sound in **ship** to /*wh*/.   (whip)

Stage 8: Phoneme Reversal

Say **pitch**. (Repeat **pitch**.) Say **pitch**. (Repeat **pitch**.)
Now, change the first sound to last, and the last sound to first.   (chip)

Say **sham**. (Repeat **sham**.) Say **sham**. (Repeat **sham**.)
Now, change the first sound to last, and the last sound to first.   (mash)

Say **shop**. (Repeat **shop**.) Say **shop**. (Repeat **shop**.)
Now, change the first sound to last, and the last sound to first.   (posh)

Say **thick**. (Repeat **thick**.) Say **thick**. (Repeat **thick**.)
Now, change the first sound to last, and the last sound to first.   (kith)

Say **pack**. (Repeat **pack**.) Say **pack**. (Repeat **pack**.)
Now, change the first sound to last, and the last sound to first.   (cap)

Say **pill**. (Repeat **pill**.) Say **pill**. (Repeat **pill**.)
Now, change the first sound to last, and the last sound to first.   (lip)

Stage 9: Pig Latin

Three or four modelings may be necessary with this activity, particularly for students with a significant lack of phonemic awareness. Do not penalize students who cannot master Pig Latin.

Say **chin**. (Repeat **chin**.) Say **chin**. (Repeat **chin**.) Say **chin** without the /*ch*/.   (/*in*/)

Say /*in*/. (Repeat /*in*/.) Say /*in*/. (Repeat /*in*/.) Say /*in*/ with /*ch*/ at the end.   (/*in ch*/)

Now, say /*ay*/ at the end.   (/*in chay*/)

Say **thank**. (Repeat **thank**.) Say **thank**. (Repeat **thank**.) Say **thank** without the /*th*/. (/*ank*/)

Say /*ank*/. (Repeat /*ank*/.) Say /*ank*/. (Repeat /*ank*/.) Say /*ank*/ with /*th*/ at the end. (/*ank th*/)

Now, say /*ay*/ at the end.   (/*ank thay*/)

Say **ship**. (Repeat **ship**.) Say **ship**. (Repeat **ship**.) Say **ship** without the /*sh*/.   (/*ip*/)

Say /*ip*/. (Repeat /*ip*/.) Say /*ip*/. (Repeat /*ip*/.) Say /*ip*/ with /*sh*/ at the end.   (/*ip sh*/)

Now, say /*ay*/ at the end.   (/*ip shay*/)

Say **thick**. (Repeat **thick**.) Say **thick**. (Repeat **thick**.) Say **thick** without the /*th*/. (/*ick*/)

Say /*ick*/. (Repeat /*ick*/.) Say /*ick*/. (Repeat /*ick*/.) Say /*ick*/ with /*th*/ at the end.   (/*ick th*/)

Now, say /*ay*/ at the end.   (/*ick thay*/)

Now, say together in Pig Latin: "I can speak Pig Latin."   (Iay ancay eakspay igpay atinlay)

Suggestions for Related Activities

- Introduce some morphologic awareness activities, using familiar compound words:
    - Say **cardboard** without the **card**.   (board)
    - Say **icebox** without the **box**.   (ice)
- Introduce some syntactic awareness activities:

    Say "The choir sang." Now, change the sentence to a question. (Did the choir sing?)

Reading and Spelling Vocabulary

bath	dish	ships	thick	whiff
cash	fish	shock	thin	wish
chap	math	shop	thing	with
chat	pinch	shot	think	*are*
chill	rich	than	this	*put*
chip	shack	thank	wham	
dash	shall	that	which	

Unit 12

Phonemic Awareness Drills

These sequential, cumulative drills assess and build phonemic awareness in emerging readers and spellers. To initiate daily lessons, present portions of these drills orally—without corresponding letters. Phonemes (sounds) should be mastered before they are associated with their orthographic representations (letters). After phonemic awareness has been established for a unit's new phonology concepts, students can be introduced to the unit's new symbol-sound correspondences and its reading/spelling vocabulary.

Phonology Concepts for Unit 12

- Consonant sounds (phonemes): Review: /b/, /d/, /f/, /g/, /h/, /j/, /k/, /l/, /m/, /n/, /p/, /r/, /s/, /t/, /v/, /w/, /y/, /z/

- Consonant letters (graphemes): Review: **b**, **c**, **d**, **f**, **g**, **h**, **j**, **k**, **l**, **m**, **n**, **p**, **qu**, **r**, **s**, **t**, **v**, **w**, **x**, **y**, **z**

- Vowel sounds (phonemes):

  – Review: short /a/, short /i/, short /o/

  – New: short /e/

- Sound-letter (phoneme-grapheme) relationship: /e/ (short **e**) is represented by **e**

Stage 1: Phoneme Production/Replication

Have the students repeat this new sound:

/e/
pen, bell, shed

Stage 2: Phoneme Isolation

Say **check**. (Repeat **check**.) Say **check**. (Repeat **check**.) What's the first sound in **check**?   (/ch/)

Say **math**. (Repeat **math**.) Say **math**. (Repeat **math**.) What's the last sound in **math**?   (/th/)

Say **deck**. (Repeat **deck**.) Say **deck**. (Repeat **deck**.) What's the middle sound in **deck**?   (/e/) (short **e**)

Say **shed**. (Repeat **shed**.) Say **shed**. (Repeat **shed**.) What's the first sound in **shed**?   (/sh/)

Say **bath**. (Repeat **bath**.) Say **bath**. (Repeat **bath**.) What's the last sound in **bath**? (/*th*/)

Say **check**. (Repeat **check**.) Say **check**. (Repeat **check**.) What's the middle sound in **check**? (/*e*/) (short **e**)

Say **when**. (Repeat **when**.) Say **when**. (Repeat **when**.) What's the first sound in **when**? (/*wh*/)

Say **wish**. (Repeat **wish**.) Say **wish**. (Repeat **wish**.) What's the last sound in **wish**? (/*sh*/)

Say **them**. (Repeat **them**.) Say **them**. (Repeat **them**.) What's the middle sound in **them**? (/*e*/) (short **e**)

Say **bath**. (Repeat **bath**.) Say **bath**. (Repeat **bath**.) What's the last sound in **bath**? (/*th*/)

Say **chop**. (Repeat **chop**.) Say **chop**. (Repeat **chop**.) What's the middle sound in **chop**? (/*o*/) (short **o**)

Say **which**. (Repeat **which**.) Say **which**. (Repeat **which**.) What's the last sound in **which**? (/*ch*/)

Stage 3: Phoneme Segmentation and Counting (Spelling the Sounds)

Say **which**. (Repeat **which**.) Say **which**. (Repeat **which**.) Say the sounds in **which**. (/*wh*/ /*i*/ /*ch*/)

Say **them**. (Repeat **them**.) Say **them**. (Repeat **them**.) Say the sounds in **them**. (/*th*/ /*e*/ /*m*/)

Say **check**. (Repeat **check**.) Say **check**. (Repeat **check**.) Say the sounds in **check**. (/*ch*/ /*e*/ /*k*/)

Say **mess**. (Repeat **mess**.) Say **mess**. (Repeat **mess**.) Say the sounds in **mess**. (/*m*/ /*e*/ /*s*/)

Say **men**. (Repeat **men**.) Say **men**. (Repeat **men**.) Say the sounds in **men**. (/*m*/ /*e*/ /*n*/)

Say **tell**. (Repeat **tell**.) Say **tell**. (Repeat **tell**.) Say the sounds in **tell**. (/*t*/ /*e*/ /*l*/)

Say **beg**. (Repeat **beg**.) Say **beg**. (Repeat **beg**.) Say the sounds in **beg**. (/*b*/ /*e*/ /*g*/)

Say **shed**. (Repeat **shed**.) Say **shed**. (Repeat **shed**.) Say the sounds in **shed**. (/*sh*/ /*e*/ /*d*/)

Say **thing**. (Repeat **thing**.) Say **thing**. (Repeat **thing**.) Say the sounds in **thing**. (/*th*/ /*i*/ /*n*/ /*g*/)

Say **fell**. (Repeat **fell**.) Say **fell**. (Repeat **fell**.) Say the sounds in **fell**. (/*f*/ /*e*/ /*l*/)

After the students have been introduced to the new unit's vocabulary words, you may ask, "How many sounds in **xxx**?" "How many letters in **xxx**?"

Stage 4: Phoneme Blending

Listen and repeat. Listen and repeat: /*wh*/ /*e*/ /*n*/. (Repeat phoneme series three times.) (when)

Listen and repeat. Listen and repeat: /*sh*/ /*o*/ /*p*/. (Repeat phoneme series three times.) (shop)

Listen and repeat. Listen and repeat: /*th*/ /*e*/ /*m*/. (Repeat phoneme series three times.) (them)

Listen and repeat. Listen and repeat: /s/ /o/ /k/. (Repeat phoneme series three times.)   (sock)

Listen and repeat. Listen and repeat: /ch/ /i/ /p/. (Repeat phoneme series three times.)   (chip)

Listen and repeat. Listen and repeat: /b/ /e/ /l/. (Repeat phoneme series three times.)   (bell)

Stage 5: Rhyming

Say **ten**. (Repeat **ten**.) Say **ten**. (Repeat **ten**.)
Say a word that rhymes with **ten**.   (hen, den, men)

Say **bell**. (Repeat **bell**.) Say **bell**. (Repeat **bell**.)
Say a word that rhymes with **bell**.   (tell, dell, sell)

Say **check**. (Repeat **check**.) Say **check**. (Repeat **check**.)
Say a word that rhymes with **check**.   (deck, neck, peck)

Say **when**. (Repeat **when**.) Say **when**. (Repeat **when**.)
Say a word that rhymes with **when**.   (pen, then, ten)

Say **yes**. (Repeat **yes**.) Say **yes**. (Repeat **yes**.)
Say a word that rhymes with **yes**.   (dress, less, mess)

Say **fed**. (Repeat **fed**.) Say **fed**. (Repeat **fed**.)
Say a word that rhymes with **fed**.   (bed, red, led)

Say **bang**. (Repeat **bang**.) Say **bang**. (Repeat **bang**.)
Say a word that rhymes with **bang**.   (hang, rang, sang)

Say **sink**. (Repeat **sink**.) Say **sink**. (Repeat **sink**.)
Say a word that rhymes with **sink**.   (link, mink, pink)

Stage 6: Phoneme Deletion

Say **chill**. (Repeat **chill**.) Say **chill**. (Repeat **chill**.) Say **chill** without the /ch/.   (/il/)

Say **bell**. (Repeat **bell**.) Say **bell**. (Repeat **bell**.) Say **bell** without the /b/.   (/el/)

Say **bed**. (Repeat **bed**.) Say **bed**. (Repeat **bed**.) Say **bed** without the /b/.   (/ed/)

Say **when**. (Repeat **when**.) Say **when**. (Repeat **when**.) Say **when** without the /wh/. (/en/)

Say **shall**. (Repeat **shall**.) Say **shall**. (Repeat **shall**.) Say **shall** without the /sh/.   (/al/)

Say **than**. (Repeat **than**.) Say **than**. (Repeat **than**.) Say **than** without the /th/.   (/an/)

Say **shed**. (Repeat **shed**.) Say **shed**. (Repeat **shed**.) Say **shed** without the /sh/.   (/ed/)

Say **chop**. (Repeat **chop**.) Say **chop**. (Repeat **chop**.) Say **chop** without the /ch/.   (/op/)

Say **mash**. (Repeat **mash**.) Say **mash**. (Repeat **mash**.) Say **mash** without the /m/. (/ash/)

Say **that**. (Repeat **that**.) Say **that**. (Repeat **that**.) Say **that** without the /<u>th</u>/.   (/at/)

Say **pen**. (Repeat **pen**.) Say **pen**. (Repeat **pen**.) Say **pen** without the /p/.   (/en/)

Say **hem**. (Repeat **hem**.) Say **hem**. (Repeat **hem**.) Say **hem** without the /h/.   (/em/)

Stage 7: Phoneme Substitution

Say **red**. (Repeat **red**.) Say **red**. (Repeat **red**.) Now, change the first sound in **red** to /sh/.   (shed)

Say **red**. (Repeat **red**.) Say **red**. (Repeat **red**.) Now, change the first sound in **red** to /w/.   (wed)

Say **thick**. (Repeat **thick**.) Say **thick**. (Repeat **thick**.) Now, change the first sound in **thick** to /ch/.   (chick)

Say **well**. (Repeat **well**.) Say **well**. (Repeat **well**.) Now, change the first sound in **well** to /y/.   (yell)

Say **shop**. (Repeat **shop**.) Say **shop**. (Repeat **shop**.) Now, change the first sound in **shop** to /ch/.   (chop)

Say **when**. (Repeat **when**.) Say **when**. (Repeat **when**.) Now, change the first sound in **when** to /th/.   (then)

Advancement: After initial phoneme(s), substitute final phoneme(s) and medial phoneme(s):

Say **pill**. (Repeat **pill**.) Say **pill**. (Repeat **pill**.) Now, change the last sound in **pill** to /k/.   (pick)

Say **shack**. (Repeat **shack**.) Say **shack**. (Repeat **shack**.) Now, change the middle sound in **shack** to /o/.   (shock)

Say **chap**. (Repeat **chap**.) Say **chap**. (Repeat **chap**.) Now, change the last sound in **chap** to /t/.   (chat)

Say **red**. (Repeat **red**.) Say **red**. (Repeat **red**.) Now, change the middle sound in **red** to /o/.   (rod)

Say **rod**. (Repeat **rod**.) Say **rod**. (Repeat **rod**.) Now, change the middle sound in **rod** to /e/.   (red)

Say **ship**. (Repeat **ship**.) Say **ship**. (Repeat **ship**.) Now, change the middle sound in **ship** to /o/.   (shop)

Say **ship**. (Repeat **ship**.) Say **ship**. (Repeat **ship**.) Now, change the first sound in **ship** to /wh/.   (whip)

Stage 8: Phoneme Reversal

Say **ten**. (Repeat **ten**.) Say **ten**. (Repeat **ten**.)
Now, change the first sound to last, and the last sound to first.   (net)

Say **sell**. (Repeat **sell**.) Say **sell**. (Repeat **sell**.)
Now, change the first sound to last, and the last sound to first.   (less)

Say **dock**. (Repeat **dock**.) Say **dock**. (Repeat **dock**.)
Now, change the first sound to last, and the last sound to first.   (cod)

Say **tell**. (Repeat **tell**.) Say **tell**. (Repeat **tell**.)
Now, change the first sound to last, and the last sound to first.   (let)

Say **Ned**. (Repeat **Ned**.) Say **Ned**. (Repeat **Ned**.)
Now, change the first sound to last, and the last sound to first.   (den)

Say **pack**. (Repeat **pack**.) Say **pack**. (Repeat **pack**.)
Now, change the first sound to last, and the last sound to first.   (cap)

Say **mash**. (Repeat **mash**.) Say **mash**. (Repeat **mash**.)
Now, change the first sound to last, and the last sound to first.   (sham)

Stage 9: Pig Latin

Three or four modelings may be necessary with this activity, particularly for students with a significant lack of phonemic awareness. Do not penalize students who cannot master Pig Latin.

Say **them**. (Repeat **them**.) Say **them**. (Repeat **them**.) Say **them** without the /<u>th</u>/.   (/em/)

Say /em/. (Repeat /em/.) Say /em/. (Repeat /em/.) Say /em/ with /th/ at the end.   (/em th/)

Now, say /ay/ at the end.   (/em thay/)

Say **when**. (Repeat **when**.) Say **when**. (Repeat **when**.) Say **when** without the /wh/.   (/en/)

Say /en/. (Repeat /en/.) Say /en/. (Repeat /en/.) Say /en/ with /wh/ at the end.   (/en wh/)

Now, say /ay/ at the end.   (/en whay/)

Say **mess**. (Repeat **mess**.) Say **mess**. (Repeat **mess**.) Say **mess** without the /m/.   (/es/)

Say /es/. (Repeat /es/.) Say /es/. (Repeat /es/.) Say /es/ with /m/ at the end.   (/es m/)

Now, say /ay/ at the end.   (/es may/)

Say **check**. (Repeat **check**.) Say **check**. (Repeat **check**.) Say **check** without the /ch/.   (/ek/)

Say /ek/. (Repeat /ek/.) Say /ek/. (Repeat /ek/.) Say /ek/ with /ch/ at the end.   (/ek ch/)

Now, say /ay/ at the end.   (/ek chay/)

Now, say together in Pig Latin: "I can speak Pig Latin."   (Iay ancay eakspay igpay atinlay)

Suggestions for Related Activities

- Create possible single-syllable English words. Have the students work individually or in groups, using:

    - The four previously mastered short vowels: <u>a</u>, <u>e</u>, <u>i</u>, and <u>o</u>

    - All of the consonant letters

    - Previously mastered spelling rules: <u>-ck</u> for /k/; <u>qu</u> for /kw/; <u>x</u> for /ks/; <u>s</u> for /z/; and doubling <u>-ll</u>, <u>-ff</u>, <u>-ss</u>, and <u>-zz</u> after short vowels at the ends of words

    - Consonant digraphs <u>ch</u>, <u>th</u>, <u>sh</u>, and <u>wh</u>

- Introduce some morphologic awareness activities:

    - Say **sidekick** without the **side**.   (kick)

    - Say **bedroom** without the **bed**.   (room)

- Introduce some syntactic awareness activities:

    - Supply some simple sentences (e.g., "I helped her.") and have students supply a "when," then a "how," then a "where"—thereby introducing the procedure for sentence expansion in English.

    - Say "Aaron sat here yesterday morning." Now, change the sentence to a question. (Did Aaron sit here yesterday morning?)

Reading/Spelling Vocabulary

bed	Ken	nets	ten	yes
beg	led	pen	them	yet
bell	leg	pet	then	
Bell	less	red	vet	*could*
bet	let	sell	well	*should*
chess	men	set	Wells	*would*
fell	mess	shell	wet	
get	met	Ted	when	
Jen	Nell	tell	yell	

Unit 13

Phonemic Awareness Drills

These sequential, cumulative drills assess and build phonemic awareness in emerging readers and spellers. To initiate daily lessons, present portions of these drills orally—without corresponding letters. Phonemes (sounds) should be mastered before they are associated with their orthographic representations (letters). After phonemic awareness has been established for a unit's new phonology concepts, students can be introduced to the unit's new symbol-sound correspondences and its reading/spelling vocabulary.

Phonology Concepts for Unit 13

- Consonant sounds (phonemes): Review: /b/, /d/, /f/, /g/, /h/, /j/, /k/, /l/, /m/, /n/, /p/, /r/, /s/, /t/, /v/, /w/, /y/, /z/

- Consonant letters (graphemes): Review: **b**, **c**, **d**, **f**, g, **h**, j, **k**, **l**, **m**, **n**, **p**, **qu**, **r**, **s**, **t**, **v**, **w**, **x**, **y**, **z**

- Vowel sounds (phonemes):

  - Review: short /a/, short /i/, short /o/, short /e/

- New: initial consonant blends: **bl-**, **gl-**, **cl-**, **pl-**, **fl-**, **sl-**, **br-**, **fr-**, **tr-**, **cr-**, **dr-**, **gr-**, **pr-**, **sc-**, **sm-**, **sn-**, **sp-**, **sk-**, **st-**, **squ-**, **sw-**, **tw-**, **dw-**, **shr-**, **thr-**

  - At the beginnings of words, initial consonant blends represent two different consonant phonemes.

Stage 1: Phoneme Production/Replication

- Have the students repeat each consonant blend:

  - /bl/, /gl/, /cl/, /pl/, /fl/, /sl/ (**-l** blends)

  - /br/, /fr/, /tr/, /cr/, /dr/, /gr/, /pr/, /shr/, /thr/ (**-r** blends)

  - /sc/, /sm/, /sn/, /sp/, /sk/, /st/, /squ/ (**s-** blends)

  - /sw/, /tw/, /dw/ (**-w** blends)

Stage 2: Phoneme Isolation

Say **black**. (Repeat **black**.) Say **black**. (Repeat **black**.) What's the first blend in **black**?   (/bl/)

Say **glass**. (Repeat **glass**.) Say **glass**. (Repeat **glass**.) What's the first blend in **glass**?   (/gl/)

Say **clang**. (Repeat **clang**.) Say **clang**. (Repeat **clang**.) What's the first blend in **clang**? *(/cl/)*

Say **brick**. (Repeat **brick**.) Say **brick**. (Repeat **brick**.) What's the first blend in **brick**? *(/br/)*

Say **fresh**. (Repeat **fresh**.) Say **fresh**. (Repeat **fresh**.) What's the first blend in **fresh**? *(/fr/)*

Say **trick**. (Repeat **trick**.) Say **trick**. (Repeat **trick**.) What's the first blend in **trick**? *(/tr/)*

Say **crop**. (Repeat **crop**.) Say **crop**. (Repeat **crop**.) What's the first blend in **crop**? *(/cr/)*

Say **prom**. (Repeat **prom**.) Say **prom**. (Repeat **prom**.) What's the first blend in **prom**? *(/pr/)*

Say **smell**. (Repeat **smell**.) Say **smell**. (Repeat **smell**.) What's the first blend in **smell**? *(/sm/)*

Say **skin**. (Repeat **skin**.) Say **skin**. (Repeat **skin**.) What's the first blend in **skin**? *(/sk/)*

Say **step**. (Repeat **step**.) Say **step**. (Repeat **step**.) What's the first blend in **step**? *(/st/)*

Say **twin**. (Repeat **twin**.) Say **twin**. (Repeat **twin**.) What's the first blend in **twin**? *(/tw/)*

Stage 3: Phoneme Segmentation and Counting (Spelling the Sounds)

Say **clip**. (Repeat **clip**.) Say **clip**. (Repeat **clip**.) Say the sounds in **clip**. *(/k/ /l/ /i/ /p/)*

Say **trash**. (Repeat **trash**.) Say **trash**. (Repeat **trash**.) Say the sounds in **trash**. *(/t/ /r/ /a/ /sh/)*

Say **flag**. (Repeat **flag**.) Say **flag**. (Repeat **flag**.) Say the sounds in **flag**. *(/f/ /l/ /a/ /g/)*

Say **clam**. (Repeat **clam**.) Say **clam**. (Repeat **clam**.) Say the sounds in **clam**. *(/k/ /l/ /a/ /m/)*

Say **slang**. (Repeat **slang**.) Say **slang**. (Repeat **slang**.) Say the sounds in **slang**. *(/s/ /l/ /a/ /n/ /g/)*

Say **brass**. (Repeat **brass**.) Say **brass**. (Repeat **brass**.) Say the sounds in **brass**. *(/b/ /r/ /a/ /s/)*

Say **bring**. (Repeat **bring**.) Say **bring**. (Repeat **bring**.) Say the sounds in **bring**. *(/b/ /r/ /i/ /n/ /g/)*

Say **snack**. (Repeat **snack**.) Say **snack**. (Repeat **snack**.) Say the sounds in **snack**. *(/s/ /n/ /a/ /k/)*

Say **swish**. (Repeat **swish**.) Say **swish**. (Repeat **swish**.) Say the sounds in **swish**. *(/s/ /w/ /i/ /sh/)*

After the students have been introduced to the new unit's vocabulary words, you may ask, "How many sounds in **xxx**?" "How many letters in **xxx**?"

Stage 4: Phoneme Blending

Listen and repeat. Listen and repeat: /s/ /n/ /a/ /p/. (Repeat phoneme series three times.)   (snap)

Listen and repeat. Listen and repeat: /s/ /m/ /o/ /g/. (Repeat phoneme series three times.)   (smog)

Listen and repeat. Listen and repeat: /s/ /w/ /a/ /m/. (Repeat phoneme series three times.)   (swam)

Listen and repeat. Listen and repeat: /k/ /r/ /a/ /k/. (Repeat phoneme series three times.)   (crack)

Listen and repeat. Listen and repeat: /sh/ /r/ /i/ /n/ /k/. (Repeat phoneme series three times.)   (shrink)

Listen and repeat. Listen and repeat: /d/ /w/ /e/ /l/. (Repeat phoneme series three times.)   (dwell)

Stage 5: Rhyming

Say **slick**. (Repeat **slick**.) Say **slick**. (Repeat **slick**.)
Say a word that rhymes with **slick**.   (pick, trick, stick)

Say **clam**. (Repeat **clam**.) Say **clam**. (Repeat **clam**.)
Say a word that rhymes with **clam**.   (ham, cram, slam)

Say **blot**. (Repeat **blot**.) Say **blot**. (Repeat **blot**.)
Say a word that rhymes with **blot**.   (clot, trot, shot)

Say **swell**. (Repeat **swell**.) Say **swell**. (Repeat **swell**.)
Say a word that rhymes with **swell**.   (fell, tell, jell)

Say **clink**. (Repeat **clink**.) Say **clink**. (Repeat **clink**.)
Say a word that rhymes with **clink**.   (pink, sink, link)

Say **sled**. (Repeat **sled**.) Say **sled**. (Repeat **sled**.)
Say a word that rhymes with **sled**.   (bled, red, fed)

Say **press**. (Repeat **press**.) Say **press**. (Repeat **press**.)
Say a word that rhymes with **press**.   (dress, mess, less)

Say **trim**. (Repeat **trim**.) Say **trim**. (Repeat **trim**.)
Say a word that rhymes with **trim**.   (him, brim, skim)

Stage 6: Phoneme Deletion

(Instructor: To delete a phoneme in this series, some initial consonant blends must be split.)

Say **clot**. (Repeat **clot**.) Say **clot**. (Repeat **clot**.) Say **clot** without the /k/.   (/lot/)

Say **trap**. (Repeat **trap**.) Say **trap**. (Repeat **trap**.) Say **trap** without the /t/.   (/rap/)

Say **clot**. (Repeat **clot**.) Say **clot**. (Repeat **clot**.) Say **clot** without the /l/.   (/cot/)

Say **spill**. (Repeat **spill**.) Say **spill**. (Repeat **spill**.) Say **spill** without the /s/.   (/pill/)

Say **snap**. (Repeat **snap**.) Say **snap**. (Repeat **snap**.) Say **snap** without the /s/.   (/nap/)

Say **stop**. (Repeat **stop**.) Say **stop**. (Repeat **stop**.) Say **stop** without the /t/.   (/sop/)

Say **snap**. (Repeat **snap**.) Say **snap**. (Repeat **snap**.) Say **snap** without the /n/.   (/sap/)

Say **black**. (Repeat **black**.) Say **black**. (Repeat **black**.) Say **black** without the /l/.   (/back/)

Say **flog**. (Repeat **flog**.) Say **flog**. (Repeat **flog**.) Say **flog** without the /f/.   (/log/)

Say **trim**. (Repeat **trim**.) Say **trim**. (Repeat **trim**.) Say **trim** without the /t/.   (/rim/)

Sat **flog**. (Repeat **flog**.) Say **flog**. (Repeat **flog**.) Say **flog** without the /l/.   (/fog/)

Say **swell**. (Repeat **swell**.) Say **swell**. (Repeat **swell**.) Say **swell** without the /s/.   (/well/)

Stage 7: Phoneme Substitution

(Instructor: In this series, the initial consonant blend must be split to form a different blend.)

Say **crash**. (Repeat **crash**.) Say **crash**. (Repeat **crash**.) Now, change the first sound in **crash** to /t/.   (trash)

Say **track**. (Repeat **track**.) Say **track**. (Repeat **track**.) Now, change the first sound in **track** to /k/.   (crack)

Say **frill**. (Repeat **frill**.) Say **frill**. (Repeat **frill**.) Now, change the first sound in **frill** to /g/.   (grill)

Say **slob**. (Repeat **slob**.) Say **slob**. (Repeat **slob**.) Now, change the first sound in **slob** to /b/.   (blob)

Say **crash**. (Repeat **crash**.) Say **crash**. (Repeat **crash**.) Now, change the first sound in **crash** to /t/.   (trash)

Say **drab**. (Repeat **drab**.) Say **drab**. (Repeat **drab**.) Now, change the first sound in **drab** to /k/.   (crab)

Say **grip**. (Repeat **grip**.) Say **grip**. (Repeat **grip**.) Now, change the first sound in **grip** to /t/.   (trip)

Say **trod**. (Repeat **trod**.) Say **trod**. (Repeat **trod**.) Now, change the first sound in **trod** to /p/.   (prod)

Say **prop**. (Repeat **prop**.) Say **prop**. (Repeat **prop**.) Now, change the first sound in **prop** to /k/.   (crop)

Say **dress**. (Repeat **dress**.) Say **dress**. (Repeat **dress**.) Now, change the first sound in **dress** to /p/.   (press)

Say **black**. (Repeat **black**.) Say **black**. (Repeat **black**.) Now, change the first sound in **black** to /s/.   (slack)

Say **slam**. (Repeat **slam**.) Say **slam**. (Repeat **slam**.) Now, change the first sound in **slam** to /k/.   (clam)

Say **drag**. (Repeat **drag**.) Say **drag**. (Repeat **drag**.) Now, change the first sound in **drag** to /b/.   (brag)

Stage 8: Phoneme Reversal

Say **drop**. (Repeat **drop**.) Say **drop**. (Repeat **drop**.)
Now, change the first sound to last, and the last sound to first.   (prod)

Say **brad**. (Repeat **brad**.) Say **brad**. (Repeat **brad**.)
Now, change the first sound to last, and the last sound to first.   (drab)

Say **class**. (Repeat **class**.) Say **class**. (Repeat **class**.)
Now, change the first sound to last, and the last sound to first.   (slack)

Say **crib**. (Repeat **crib**.) Say **crib**. (Repeat **crib**.)
Now, change the first sound to last, and the last sound to first.   (brick)

Say **cliff**. (Repeat **cliff**.) Say **cliff**. (Repeat **cliff**.)
Now, change the first sound to last, and the last sound to first.   (flick)

Say **pack**. (Repeat **pack**.) Say **pack**. (Repeat **pack**.)
Now, change the first sound to last, and the last sound to first.   (cap)

Say **mash**. (Repeat **mash**.) Say **mash**. (Repeat **mash**.)
Now, change the first sound to last, and the last sound to first.   (sham)

Stage 9: Pig Latin

Three or four modelings may be necessary with this activity, particularly for students with a significant lack of phonemic awareness. Do not penalize students who cannot master Pig Latin.

Say **sled**. (Repeat **sled**.) Say **sled**. (Repeat **sled**.) Say **sled** without the /sl/.   (/ed/)

Say /ed/. (Repeat /ed/.) Say /ed/. (Repeat /ed/.) Say /ed/ with /sl/ at the end.   (/ed sl/)

Now, say /ay/ at the end.   (/ed slay/)

Say **fresh**. (Repeat **fresh**.) Say **fresh**. (Repeat **fresh**.) Say **fresh** without the /fr/.   (/esh/)

Say /esh/. (Repeat /esh/.) Say /esh/. (Repeat /esh/.) Say /esh/ with /fr/ at the end.   (/esh fr/)

Now, say /ay/ at the end.   (/esh fray/)

Say **broth**. (Repeat **broth**.) Say **broth**. (Repeat **broth**.) Say **broth** without the /br/. (/oth/)

Say /oth/. (Repeat /oth/.) Say /oth/. (Repeat /oth/.) Say /oth/ with /br/ at the end.   (/oth br/)

Now, say /ay/ at the end.   (/oth bray/)

Say **skill**. (Repeat **skill**.) Say **skill**. (Repeat **skill**.) Say **skill** without the /sk/.   (/ill/)

Say /ill/. (Repeat /ill/.) Say /ill/. (Repeat /ill/.) Say /ill/ with /sk/ at the end.   (/ill sk/)

Now, say /ay/ at the end.   (/ill skay/)

Now, say together in Pig Latin: "I can speak Pig Latin."   (Iay ancay eakspay igpay atinlay)

Suggestions for Related Activities

- Create possible single-syllable English words. Have students work individually or in groups, using:

  - The four previously mastered short vowels: **a**, **e**, **i**, and **o**

  - All of the consonant letters

  - Previously mastered spelling rules: **-ck** for /*k*/; **qu** for /*kw*/; **x** for /*ks*/; **s** for /*z*/; and doubling **-ll**, **-ff**, **-ss**, and **-zz** after short vowels at the ends of words

  - Consonant digraphs **ch**, **th**, **sh**, and **wh**

- Introduce some morphologic awareness activities:

  - Say **backfield** without the **field**.   (back)

  - Say **setup** without the **up**.   (set)

- Introduce some syntactic awareness activities:

  - Supply some simple sentences (e.g., "I helped her.") and have students supply a "when," then a "how," then a "where"—thereby introducing the procedure for sentence expansion in English.

  - Say "The nurse prepared the bandage." Now, change the sentence to a question. (Did the nurse prepare the bandage?)

Reading/Spelling Vocabulary

black	clock	flat	shrill	spot	thrill
blocks	crab	flock	skill	stack	trash
Brad	crash	fresh	slash	stand	trick
brag	cross	glad	slim	stick	trip
brick	drag	glib	smash	sticks	twin
brim	drinks	grill	smell	stiff	which
brisk	drop	plan	snack	still	*they*
clam	flag	plot	snap	stink	*your*
clap	flap	prick	sniff	swim	
class	flash	shrank	spill	thong	

Unit 14

Phonemic Awareness Drills

These sequential, cumulative drills assess and build phonemic awareness in emerging readers and spellers. To initiate daily lessons, present portions of these drills orally—without corresponding letters. Phonemes (sounds) should be mastered before they are associated with their orthographic representations (letters). After phonemic awareness has been established for a unit's new phonology concepts, students can be introduced to the unit's new symbol-sound correspondences and its reading/spelling vocabulary.

Phonology Concepts for Unit 14

- Consonant sounds (phonemes): Review: /b/, /d/, /f/, /g/, /h/, /j/, /k/, /l/, /m/, /n/, /p/, /r/, /s/, /t/, /v/, /w/, /y/, /z/

- Consonant letters (graphemes): Review: **b**, **c**, **d**, **f**, **g**, **h**, **j**, **k**, **l**, **m**, **n**, **p**, **qu**, **r**, **s**, **t**, **v**, **w**, **x**, **y**, **z**

- Initial consonant blends: Review: **bl-**, **gl-**, **cl-**, **pl-**, **fl-**, **sl-**, **br-**, **fr-**, **tr-**, **cr-**, **dr-**, **gr-**, **pr-**, **shr-**, **thr-**, **sc-**, **sm-**, **sn-**, **sp-**, **sk-**, **st-**, **squ-**, **sw-**, **tw-**, **dw-**

- Vowel sounds (phonemes):

  - Review: short /a/, short /i/, short /o/, short /e/

  - New: short /u/

  - Sound-letter (phoneme-grapheme) relationship: /u/ (short **u**) is represented by **u**

Stage 1: Phoneme Production/Replication

Have the students repeat this new vowel sound: /u/ (short **u**)

Stage 2: Phoneme Isolation

Say **glum**. (Repeat **glum**.) Say **glum**. (Repeat **glum**.) What's the first sound in **glum**?   (/g/)

Say **bus**. (Repeat **bus**.) Say **bus**. (Repeat **bus**.) What's the last sound in **bus**?   (/s/)

Say **duck**. (Repeat **duck**.) Say **duck**. (Repeat **duck**.) What's the middle sound
in **duck**?   (/u/) (short **u**)

Say **shut**. (Repeat **shut**.) Say **shut**. (Repeat **shut**.) What's the first sound in **shut**?   (/sh/)

Say **thud**. (Repeat **thud**.) Say **thud**. (Repeat **thud**.) What's the first sound in **thud**?   (/th/)

Say **chuck**. (Repeat **chuck**.) Say **chuck**. (Repeat **chuck**.) What's the middle sound
in **chuck**?   (/u/) (short **u**)

Say **when**. (Repeat **when**.) Say **when**. (Repeat **when**.) What's the first sound in **when**? (/wh/)

Say **wish**. (Repeat **wish**.) Say **wish**. (Repeat **wish**.) What's the last sound in **wish**? (/sh/)

Say **but**. (Repeat **but**.) Say **but**. (Repeat **but**.) What's the middle sound in **but**? (/u/) (short **u**)

Say **zap**. (Repeat **zap**.) Say **zap**. (Repeat **zap**.) What's the first sound in **zap**? (/z/)

Say **cup**. (Repeat **cup**.) Say **cup**. (Repeat **cup**.) What's the middle sound in **cup**? (/u/) (short **u**)

Say **which**. (Repeat **which**.) Say **which**. (Repeat **which**.) What's the last sound in **which**? (/ch/)

Stage 3. Phoneme Segmentation and Counting (Spelling the Sounds)

Say **snug**. (Repeat **snug**.) Say **snug**. (Repeat **snug**.) Say the sounds in **snug**. (/s/ /n/ /u/ /g/)

Say **truck**. (Repeat **truck**.) Say **truck**. (Repeat **truck**.) Say the sounds in **truck**. (/t/ /r/ /u/ /k/)

Say **plus**. (Repeat **plus**.) Say **plus**. (Repeat **plus**.) Say the sounds in **plus**. (/p/ /l/ /u/ /s/)

Say **brush**. (Repeat **brush**.) Say **brush**. (Repeat **brush**.) Say the sounds in **brush**. (/b/ /r/ /u/ /sh/)

Say **slum**. (Repeat **slum**.) Say **slum**. (Repeat **slum**.) Say the sounds in **slum**. (/s/ /l/ /u/ /m/)

Say **flunk**. (Repeat **flunk**.) Say **flunk**. (Repeat **flunk**.) Say the sounds in **flunk**. (/f/ /l/ /u/ /n/ /k/)

Say **drum**. (Repeat **drum**.) Say **drum**. (Repeat **drum**.) Say the sounds in **drum**. (/d/ /r/ /u/ /m/)

Say **shrub**. (Repeat **shrub**.) Say **shrub**. (Repeat **shrub**.) Say the sounds in **shrub**. (/sh/ /r/ /u/ /b/)

After the students have been introduced to the new unit's vocabulary words, you may ask, "How many sounds in **xxx**?" "How many letters in **xxx**?"

Stage 4: Phoneme Blending

Listen and repeat. Listen and repeat: /sh/ /u/ /t/. (Repeat phoneme series three times.) (shut)

Listen and repeat. Listen and repeat: /s/ /p/ /u/ /n/. (Repeat phoneme series three times.) (spun)

Listen and repeat. Listen and repeat: /s/ /u/ /m/. (Repeat phoneme series three times.) (sum)

Listen and repeat. Listen and repeat: /k/ /l/ /u/ /b/. (Repeat phoneme series three times.) (club)

Listen and repeat. Listen and repeat: /b/ /r/ /u/ /sh/. (Repeat phoneme series three times.) (brush)

Listen and repeat. Listen and repeat: /t/ /w/ /i/ /n/. (Repeat phoneme series three times.) (twin)

Stage 5: Rhyming

Say **stub**. (Repeat **stub**.) Say **stub**. (Repeat **stub**.)
Say a word that rhymes with **stub**.   (rub, hub, grub)

Say **pun**. (Repeat **pun**.) Say **pun**. (Repeat **pun**.)
Say a word that rhymes with **pun**.   (run, bun, fun)

Say **up**. (Repeat **up**.) Say **up**. (Repeat **up**.)
Say a word that rhymes with **up**.   (pup, cup, sup)

Say **plum**. (Repeat **plum**.) Say **plum**. (Repeat **plum**.)
Say a word that rhymes with **plum**.   (hum, sum, bum)

Say **shun**. (Repeat **shun**.) Say **shun**. (Repeat **shun**.)
Say a word that rhymes with **shun**.   (bun, fun, pun)

Say **brad**. (Repeat **brad**.) Say **brad**. (Repeat **brad**.)
Say a word that rhymes with **brad**.   (had, lad, sad)

Say **thug**. (Repeat **thug**.) Say **thug**. (Repeat **thug**.)
Say a word that rhymes with **thug**.   (mug, bug, dug)

Say **brag**. (Repeat **brag**.) Say **brag**. (Repeat **brag**.)
Say a word that rhymes with **brag**.   (sag, bag, drag)

Stage 6: Phoneme Deletion

Say **glum**. (Repeat **glum**.) Say **glum**. (Repeat **glum**.) Say **glum** without the /g/.   (/lum/)

Say **grub**. (Repeat **grub**.) Say **grub**. (Repeat **grub**.) Say **grub** without the /g/.   (/rub/)

Say **spun**. (Repeat **spun**.) Say **spun**. (Repeat **spun**.) Say **spun** without the /s/.   (/pun/)

Say **club**. (Repeat **club**.) Say **club**. (Repeat **club**.) Say **club** without the /l/.   (/cub/)

Say **clam**. (Repeat **clam**.) Say **clam**. (Repeat **clam**.) Say **clam** without the /l/.   (/cam/)

Say **stop**. (Repeat **stop**.) Say **stop**. (Repeat **stop**.) Say **stop** without the /s/.   (/top/)

Say **drug**. (Repeat **drug**.) Say **drug**. (Repeat **drug**.) Say **drug** without the /r/.   (/dug/)

Say **spun**. (Repeat **spun**.) Say **spun**. (Repeat **spun**.) Say **spun** without the /p/.   (/sun/)

Say **mash**. (Repeat **mash**.) Say **mash**. (Repeat **mash**.) Say **mash** without the /m/.   (/ash/)

Say **grab**. (Repeat **grab**.) Say **grab**. (Repeat **grab**.) Say **grab** without the /r/.   (/gab/)

Say **plug**. (Repeat **plug**.) Say **plug**. (Repeat **plug**.) Say **plug** without the /p/.   (/lug/)

Say **slum**. (Repeat **slum**.) Say **slum**. (Repeat **slum**.) Say **slum** without the /l/.   (/sum/)

Stage 7: Phoneme Substitution

Say **gum**. (Repeat **gum**.) Say **gum**. (Repeat **gum**.) Now, change the first sound in **gum** to /s/. (sum)

Say **cluck**. (Repeat **cluck**.) Say **cluck**. (Repeat **cluck**.) Now, change the first sound in
cluck to /p/.   (pluck)

Say **bun**. (Repeat **bun**.) Say **bun**. (Repeat **bun**.) Now, change the first sound in **bun** to /sh/.   (shun)

Say **clam**. (Repeat **clam**.) Say **clam**. (Repeat **clam**.) Now, change the first sound in **clam** to /s/.   (slam)

Say **bud**. (Repeat **bud**.) Say **bud**. (Repeat **bud**.) Now, change the first sound in **bud** to /th/.   (thud)

Say **bug**. (Repeat **bug**.) Say **bug**. (Repeat **bug**.) Now, change the first sound in **bug** to /d/.   (dug)

Advancement: After initial phoneme(s), substitute final phoneme(s) and medial phoneme(s):

Say **pill**. (Repeat **pill**.) Say **pill**. (Repeat **pill**.) Now, change the first sound in **pill** to /k/.   (kill)

Say **duck**. (Repeat **duck**.) Say **duck**. (Repeat **duck**.) Now, change the middle sound in
duck to /o/.   (dock)

Say **chip**. (Repeat **chip**.) Say **chip**. (Repeat **chip**.) Now, change the last sound in **chip** to /n/.   (chin)

Say **tab**. (Repeat **tab**.) Say **tab**. (Repeat **tab**.) Now, change the middle sound in **tab** to /u/.   (tub)

Say **fad**. (Repeat **fad**.) Say **fad**. (Repeat **fad**.) Now, change the middle sound in **fad** to /e/.   (fed)

Say **shot**. (Repeat **shot**.) Say **shot**. (Repeat **shot**.) Now, change the middle sound in **shot** to /u/. (shut)

Say **ship**. (Repeat **ship**.) Say **ship**. (Repeat **ship**.) Now, change the first sound in **ship** to /wh/.   (whip)

Stage 8: Phoneme Reversal

Say **gum**. (Repeat **gum**.) Say **gum**. (Repeat **gum**.)
Now, change the first sound to last, and the last sound to first.   (mug)

Say **tell**. (Repeat **tell**.) Say **tell**. (Repeat **tell**.)
Now, change the first sound to last, and the last sound to first.   (let)

Say **gull**. (Repeat **gull**.) Say **gull**. (Repeat **gull**.)
Now, change the first sound to last, and the last sound to first.   (lug)

Say **sap**. (Repeat **sap**.) Say **sap**. (Repeat **sap**.)
Now, change the first sound to last, and the last sound to first.   (pass)

Say **cud**. (Repeat **cud**.) Say **cud**. (Repeat **cud**.)
Now, change the first sound to last, and the last sound to first.   (duck)

Say **nub**. (Repeat **nub**.) Say **nub**. (Repeat **nub**.)
Now, change the first sound to last, and the last sound to first.   (bun)

Say **bus**. (Repeat **bus**.) Say **bus**. (Repeat **bus**.)
Now, change the first sound to last, and the last sound to first.   (sub)

Stage 9: Pig Latin

Three or four modelings may be necessary with this activity, particularly for students with a significant lack of phonemic awareness. Do not penalize students who cannot master Pig Latin.

Say **bluff**. (Repeat **bluff**.) Say **bluff**. (Repeat **bluff**.) Say **bluff** without the /*bl*/.   (/*uf*/)

Say /*uf*/. (Repeat /*uf*/.) Say /*uf*/. (Repeat /*uf*/.) Say /*uf*/ with /*bl*/ at the end.   (/*uf bl*/)

Now, say /*ay*/ at the end.   (/*uf blay*/)

Say **spun**. (Repeat **spun**.) Say **spun**. (Repeat **spun**.) Say **spun** without the /*sp*/.   (/*un*/)

Say /*un*/. (Repeat /*un*/.) Say /*un*/. (Repeat /*un*/.) Say /*un*/ with /*sp*/ at the end.   (/*un sp*/)

Now, say /*ay*/ at the end.   (/*un spay*/)

Say **truck**. (Repeat **truck**.) Say **truck**. (Repeat **truck**.) Say **truck** without the /*tr*/.   (/*uk*/)

Say /*uk*/. (Repeat /*uk*/.) Say /*uk*/. (Repeat /*uk*/.) Say /*uk*/ with /*tr*/ at the end.   (/*uk tr*/)

Now, say /*ay*/ at the end.   (/*uk tray*/)

Say **drum**. (Repeat **drum**.) Say **drum**. (Repeat **drum**.) Say **drum** without the /*dr*/. (/*um*/)

Say /*um*/. (Repeat /*um*/.) Say /*um*/. (Repeat /*um*/.) Say /*um*/ with /*dr*/ at the end.   (/*um dr*/)

Now, say /*ay*/ at the end.   (/*um dray*/)

Now, say together in Pig Latin: "I can speak Pig Latin."   (Iay ancay eakspay igpay atinlay)

Suggestions for Related Activities

- Create possible single-syllable English words. Have students work individually or in groups, using:

  - The four previously mastered short vowels: **a**, **e**, **i**, and **o**

  - All of the consonant letters

  - Previously mastered spelling rules: **-ck** for /*k*/; **qu** for /*kw*/; **x** for /*ks*/; **s** for /*z*/; and doubling **-ll**, **-ff**, **-ss**, and **-zz** after short vowels at the ends of words

  - Consonant digraphs **ch**, **th**, **sh**, and **wh**

- Introduce some morphologic awareness activities:

  - Say **birthday** without the **birth**.   (day)

  - Say **billfold** without the **bill**.   (fold)

- Introduce some syntactic awareness activities:

  - Supply some simple sentences (e.g., "I helped her.") and have students supply a "when," then a "how," then a "where"—thereby introducing the procedure for sentence expansion in English.

  - Say "They went to the party." Now, change the sentence to a question. (Did they go to the party?)

Reading/Spelling Vocabulary

blush	crush	gum	just	rub	too
Bud	cups	help	luck	run	truck
bugs	cut	hub	lunch	rush	tub
bunks	dull	huff	much	shrubs	up
bus	flung	hug	mud	stuck	us
but	fuss	hunch	munch	stuff	*Mr.*
Chung	grump	hush	nuts	stung	*Mrs.*
chunk	Grunch	jump	puff	such	

Unit 15

Phonemic Awareness Drills

These sequential, cumulative drills assess and build phonemic awareness in emerging readers and spellers. To initiate daily lessons, present portions of these drills orally—without corresponding letters. Phonemes (sounds) should be mastered before they are associated with their orthographic representations (letters). After phonemic awareness has been established for a unit's new phonology concepts, students are introduced to the unit's new symbol-sound correspondences and its reading/spelling vocabulary.

Phonology Concepts for Unit 15

- Consonant sounds (phonemes): Review: /b/, /d/, /f/, /g/, /h/, /j/, /k/, /l/, /m/, /n/, /p/, /r/, /s/, /t/, /v/, /w/, /y/, /z/

- Consonant letters (graphemes): Review: **b**, **c**, **d**, **f**, g, **h**, j, **k**, **l**, **m**, **n**, p, **qu**, **r**, **s**, **t**, **v**, **w**, x, y, **z**

- Initial consonant blends: Review: **bl-**, **gl-**, **cl-**, **pl-**, **fl-**, **sl-**, **br-**, **fr-**, **tr-**, **cr-**, **dr-**, **gr-**, **pr-**, **shr-**, **thr-**, **sc-**, **sm-**, **sn-**, **sp-**, **sk-**, **st-**, **squ-**, **sw-**, **tw-**, **dw-**

- Vowel sounds (phonemes): Review: short /a/, short /i/, short /o/, short /e/, short /u/

- Syllabication: New: A word has at least one vowel sound (phoneme). A word has one or more syllables. Each syllable contains one vowel sound. The number of vowel sounds in a word always equals the number of syllables in the word.

Stage 1: Syllable Rule Production/Replication

- Have the students identify the vowel phoneme in each syllable and repeat the syllabication rule.

- Have the students repeat this rule: The number of vowel sounds in a word always equals the number of syllables in the word.

Stage 2: Syllable Isolation

Say **insect**. (Repeat **insect**.) Say **insect**. (Repeat **insect**.) What's the first syllable in **insect**?   (/*in*/)

Say **campus**. (Repeat **campus**.) Say **campus**. (Repeat **campus**.) What's the first syllable in **campus**?   (/*cam*/)

Say **admit**. (Repeat **admit**.) Say **admit**. (Repeat **admit**.) What's the last syllable in **admit**?   (/*mit*/)

Say **napkin**. (Repeat **napkin**.) Say **napkin**. (Repeat **napkin**.) What's the first syllable in **napkin**?   (/*nap*/)

Say **padlock**. (Repeat **padlock**.) Say **padlock**. (Repeat **padlock**.) What's the last syllable in **padlock**? *(/lock/)*

Say **sunset**. (Repeat **sunset**.) Say **sunset**. (Repeat **sunset**.) What's the first syllable in **sunset**? *(/sun/)*

Say **splendid**. (Repeat **splendid**.) Say **splendid**. (Repeat **splendid**.) What's the first syllable in **splendid**? *(/splen/)*

Say **zigzag**. (Repeat **zigzag**.) Say **zigzag**. (Repeat **zigzag**.) What's the last syllable in **zigzag**? *(/zag/)*

Say **pigpen**. (Repeat **pigpen**.) Say **pigpen**. (Repeat **pigpen**.) What's the last syllable in **pigpen**? *(/pen/)*

Say **upset**. (Repeat **upset**.) Say **upset**. (Repeat **upset**.) What's the last syllable in **upset**? *(/set/)*

Say **fabric**. (Repeat **fabric**.) Say **fabric**. (Repeat **fabric**.) What's the first syllable in **fabric**? *(/fab/)*

Say **velvet**. (Repeat **velvet**.) Say **velvet**. (Repeat **velvet**.) What's the first syllable in **velvet**? *(/vel/)*

Say **under**. (Repeat **under**.) Say **under**. (Repeat **under**.) What's the first syllable in **under**? *(/un/)*

Say **spotless**. (Repeat **spotless**.) Say **spotless**. (Repeat **spotless**.) What's the first syllable in **spotless**? *(/spot/)*

Say **blacktop**. (Repeat **blacktop**.) Say **blacktop**. (Repeat **blacktop**.) What's the last syllable in **blacktop**? *(/top/)*

Say **express**. (Repeat **express**.) Say **express**. (Repeat **express**.) What's the first syllable in **express**? *(/ex/)*

Say **dismiss**. (Repeat **dismiss**.) Say **dismiss**. (Repeat **dismiss**.) What's the first syllable in **dismiss**? *(/dis/)*

Say **fantastic**. (Repeat **fantastic**.) Say **fantastic**. (Repeat **fantastic**.) What's the first syllable in **fantastic**? *(/fan/)*

Stage 3: Phoneme and Syllable Counting (Spelling the Sounds and Clapping Out Syllables)

Say **sunset**. (Repeat **sunset**.) Say **sunset**. (Repeat **sunset**.)
Say the sounds in **sunset**. *(/s/ /u/ /n/ /s/ /e/ /t/)*

Say **dismiss**. (Repeat **dismiss**.) Say **dismiss**. (Repeat **dismiss**.)
Say the sounds in **dismiss**. *(/d/ /i/ /s/ /m/ /i/ /s/)*

Say **credit**. (Repeat **credit**.) Say **credit**. (Repeat **credit**.)
Say the sounds in **credit**. *(/k/ /r/ /e/ /d/ /i/ /t/)*

Say **medic**. (Repeat **medic**.) Say **medic**. (Repeat **medic**.)
Say the sounds in **medic**. *(/m/ /e/ /d/ /i/ /k/)*

Say **fantastic**. (Repeat **fantastic**.) Say **fantastic**. (Repeat **fantastic**.)
Say the sounds in **fantastic**. *(/f/ /a/ /n/ /t/ /a/ /s/ /t/ /i/ /k/)*

Say **telling**. (Repeat **telling**.) Say **telling**. (Repeat **telling**.)
Say the sounds in **telling**.

(/t/ /e/ /l/ /i/ /n/ /g/)

Say **padded**. (Repeat **padded**.) Say **padded**. (Repeat **padded**.)
Say the sounds in **padded**.

(/p/ /a/ /d/ /e/ /d/)

Say **velvet**. (Repeat **velvet**.) Say **velvet**. (Repeat **velvet**.)
Say the sounds in **velvet**.

(/v/ /e/ /l/ /v/ /e/ /t/)

Say **thing**. (Repeat **thing**.) Say **thing**. (Repeat **thing**.)
Say the sounds in **thing**.

(/th/ /i/ /n/ /g/)

Say **discuss**. (Repeat **discuss**.) Say **discuss**. (Repeat **discuss**.)
Say the sounds in **discuss**.

(/d/ /i/ /s/ /c/ /u/ /s/)

After the students have been introduced to the new unit's vocabulary words, you may ask, "How many sounds in **xxx**?" "How many letters in **xxx**?"

Stage 4: Phoneme Blending

Listen and repeat. Listen and repeat: /u/ /p/ /s/ /e/ /t/.
(Repeat phoneme series three times.)

(upset)

Listen and repeat. Listen and repeat: /b/ /a/ /s/ /k/ /e/ /t/.
(Repeat phoneme series three times.)

(basket)

Listen and repeat. Listen and repeat: /p/ /l/ /a/ /s/ /t/ /i/ /k/.
(Repeat phoneme series three times.)

(plastic)

Listen and repeat. Listen and repeat: /h/ /e/ /l/ /m/ /e/ /t/.
(Repeat phoneme series three times.)

(helmet)

Listen and repeat. Listen and repeat: /m/ /u/ /f/ /i/ /n/.
(Repeat phoneme series three times.)

(muffin)

Listen and repeat. Listen and repeat: /s/ /t/ /a/ /t/ /i/ /k/.
(Repeat phoneme series three times.)

(static)

Stage 5: Rhyming

Say **bran**. (Repeat **bran**.) Say **bran**. (Repeat **bran**.)
Say a word that rhymes with **bran**.

(ban, tan, clan)

Say **swell**. (Repeat **swell**.) Say **swell**. (Repeat **swell**.)
Say a word that rhymes with **swell**.

(tell, dwell, sell)

Say **stuck**. (Repeat **stuck**.) Say **stuck**. (Repeat **stuck**.)
Say a word that rhymes with **stuck**.

(pluck, tuck, buck)

Say **when**. (Repeat **when**.) Say **when**. (Repeat **when**.)
Say a word that rhymes with **when**. (pen, then, ten)

Say **tress**. (Repeat **tress**.) Say **tress**. (Repeat **tress**.)
Say a word that rhymes with **tress**. (dress, less, mess)

Say **tread**. (Repeat **tread**.) Say **tread**. (Repeat **tread**.)
Say a word that rhymes with **tread**. (bred, red, pled)

Say **clang**. (Repeat **clang**.) Say **clang**. (Repeat **clang**.)
Say a word that rhymes with **clang**. (twang, rang, sang)

Say **stink**. (Repeat **stink**.) Say **stink**. (Repeat **stink**.)
Say a word that rhymes with **stink**. (clink, mink, pink)

Stage 6: Syllable Deletion

Say **credit**. (Repeat **credit**.) Say **credit**. (Repeat **credit**.) Say **credit** without the /cred/. (/it/)

Say **catnap**. (Repeat **catnap**.) Say **catnap**. (Repeat **catnap**.) Say **catnap** without the /nap/. (/cat/)

Say **padlock**. (Repeat **padlock**.) Say **padlock**. (Repeat **padlock**.) Say **padlock** without the /pad/. (/lock/)

Say **pigpen**. (Repeat **pigpen**.) Say **pigpen**. (Repeat **pigpen**.) Say **pigpen** without the /pig/. (/pen/)

Say **splendid**. (Repeat **splendid**.) Say **splendid**. (Repeat **splendid**.) Say **splendid** without the /did/. (/splen/)

Say **shamrock**. (Repeat **shamrock**.) Say **shamrock**. (Repeat **shamrock**.) Say **shamrock** without the /sham/. (/rock/)

Say **dismiss**. (Repeat **dismiss**.) Say **dismiss**. (Repeat **dismiss**.) Say **dismiss** without the /miss/. (/dis/)

Say **comic**. (Repeat **comic**.) Say **comic**. (Repeat **comic**.) Say **comic** without the /ic/. (/com/)

Say **frogman**. (Repeat **frogman**.) Say **frogman**. (Repeat **frogman**.) Say **frogman** without the /man/. (/frog/)

Say **locket**. (Repeat **locket**.) Say **locket**. (Repeat **locket**.) Say **locket** without the /et/. (/lock/)

Say **napkin**. (Repeat **napkin**.) Say **napkin**. (Repeat **napkin**.) Say **napkin** without the /nap/. (/kin/)

Say **admit**. (Repeat **admit**.) Say **admit**. (Repeat **admit**.) Say **admit** without the /ad/. (/mit/)

Stage 7: Syllable Substitution

Say **habit**. (Repeat **habit**.) Say **habit**. (Repeat **habit**.)
Now, change the first syllable in **habit** to /rab/. (rabbit)

Say **slingshot**. (Repeat **slingshot**.) Say **slingshot**. (Repeat **slingshot**.)
Now, change the first syllable in **slingshot** to /*hot*/.   (hotshot)

Say **picnic**. (Repeat **picnic**.) Say **picnic**. (Repeat **picnic**.)
Now, change the first syllable in **picnic** to /*pan*/.   (panic)

Say **express**. (Repeat **express**.) Say **express**. (Repeat **express**.)
Now, change the first syllable in **express** to /*im*/.   (impress)

Say **pocket**. (Repeat **pocket**.) Say **pocket**. (Repeat **pocket**.)
Now, change the first syllable in **pocket** to /*sock*/.   (socket)

Advancement: After initial syllable(s), substitute final syllable(s):

Say **catnap**. (Repeat **catnap**.) Say **catnap**. (Repeat **catnap**.)
Now, change the last syllable in **catnap** to /*nip*/.   (catnip)

Say **dismiss**. (Repeat **dismiss**.) Say **dismiss**. (Repeat **dismiss**.)
Now, change the last syllable in **dismiss** to /*cuss*/.   (discuss)

Say **enlist**. (Repeat **enlist**.) Say **enlist**. (Repeat **enlist**.)
Now, change the last syllable in **enlist** to /*trap*/.   (entrap)

Say **jacket**. (Repeat **jacket**.) Say **jacket**. (Repeat **jacket**.)
Now, change the last syllable in **jacket** to /*pot*/.   (jackpot)

Say **shipping**. (Repeat **shipping**.) Say **shipping**. (Repeat **shipping**.)
Now, change the first syllable in **shipping** to /*sing*/.   (singing)

Say **shipping**. (Repeat **shipping**.) Say **shipping**. (Repeat **shipping**.)
Now, change the last syllable in **shipping** to /*ment*/.   (shipment)

Stage 8: Phoneme Reversal

Say **ten**. (Repeat **ten**.) Say **ten**. (Repeat **ten**.)
Now, change the first sound to last, and the last sound to first.   (net)

Say **kin**. (Repeat **kin**.) Say **kin**. (Repeat **kin**.)
Now, change the first sound to last, and the last sound to first.   (nick)

Say **cod**. (Repeat **cod**.) Say **cod**. (Repeat **cod**.)
Now, change the first sound to last, and the last sound to first.   (dock)

Say **tell**. (Repeat **tell**.) Say **tell**. (Repeat **tell**.)
Now, change the first sound to last, and the last sound to first.   (let)

Say **ban**. (Repeat **ban**.) Say **ban**. (Repeat **ban**.)
Now, change the first sound to last, and the last sound to first.   (nab)

Say **pack**. (Repeat **pack**.) Say **pack**. (Repeat **pack**.)
Now, change the first sound to last, and the last sound to first.   (cap)

Say **dash**. (Repeat **dash**.) Say **dash**. (Repeat **dash**.)
Now, change the first sound to last, and the last sound to first.   (shad)

Stage 9: Pig Latin

Three or four modelings may be necessary with this activity, particularly for students with a significant lack of phonemic awareness. Do not penalize students who cannot master Pig Latin.

Say **napkin**. (Repeat **napkin**.) Say **napkin**. (Repeat **napkin**.)
Say **napkin** without the /n/.   (*/ap kin/*)

Say */apkin/*. (Repeat */apkin/*.) Say */apkin/*. (Repeat */apkin/*.)
Say */apkin/* with /n/ at the end.   (*/ap kin n/*)

Now, say */ay/* at the end.   (*/ap kin nay/*)

Say **picnic**. (Repeat **picnic**.) Say **picnic**. (Repeat **picnic**.)
Say **picnic** without the /p/.   (*/ik nik/*)

Say */iknik/*. (Repeat */iknik/*.) Say */iknik/*. (Repeat */iknik/*.)
Say */iknik/* with /p/ at the end.   (*/ik nik p/*)

Now, say */ay/* at the end.   (*/ik nik pay/*)

Say **fantastic**. (Repeat **fantastic**.) Say **fantastic**. (Repeat **fantastic**.)
Say **fantastic** without the /f/.   (*/an tas tik/*)

Say */antastik/*. (Repeat */antastik/*.) Say */antastik/*. (Repeat */antastik/*.)
Say */antastik/* with /f/ at the end.   (*/an tas tik f/*)

Now, say */ay/* at the end.   (*/an tas tik fay/*)

Say **padlock**. (Repeat **padlock**.) Say **padlock**. (Repeat **padlock**.)
Say **padlock** without the /p/.   (*/ad lok/*)

Say */adlok/*. (Repeat */adlok/*.) Say */adlok/*. (Repeat */adlok/*.)
Say */adlok/* with /p/ at the end.   (*/ad lok p/*)

Now, say */ay/* at the end.   (*/ad lok pay/*)

Now, say together in Pig Latin: "I can speak Pig Latin."   (Iay ancay eakspay igpay atinlay)

Suggestions for Related Activities

Create possible double-syllable and multisyllable English words. Have the students work individually or in groups, using:

- The four previously mastered short vowels: <u>a</u>, <u>e</u>, <u>i</u>, and <u>o</u>

- All of the consonant letters

- Previously mastered spelling rules: <u>-ck</u> for /k/; <u>qu</u> for /kw/; <u>x</u> for /ks/; <u>s</u> for /z/; and doubling <u>-ll</u>, <u>-ff</u>, <u>-ss</u>, and <u>-zz</u> after short vowels at the ends of words

- Consonant digraphs <u>ch</u>, <u>th</u>, <u>sh</u>, and <u>wh</u>

- Initial consonant blends

Reading/Spelling Vocabulary

admit	fabric	muffin	rabbit	traffic
basket	fantastic	napkin	ragbag	upset
cactus	Frogman	padlock	shamrock	velvet
campus	goblin	picnic	splendid	zigzag
cannot	insect	pigpen	sunset	*into*
catnap	jacket	plastic	talcum	
comic	locket	pockets	tickets	

Unit 16

Phonemic Awareness Drills

These sequential, cumulative drills assess and build phonemic awareness in emerging readers and spellers. To initiate daily lessons, present portions of these drills orally—without corresponding letters. Phonemes (sounds) should be mastered before they are associated with their orthographic representations (letters). After phonemic awareness has been established for a unit's new phonology concepts, students can be introduced to the unit's new symbol-sound correspondences and its reading/spelling vocabulary.

Phonology Concepts for Unit 16

- Consonant sounds (phonemes): Review: /b/, /d/, /f/, /g/, /h/, /j/, /k/, /l/, /m/, /n/, /p/, /r/, /s/, /t/, /v/, /w/, /y/, /z/

- Consonant letters (graphemes): Review: **b**, **c**, **d**, **f**, **g**, **h**, **j**, **k**, **l**, **m**, **n**, **p**, **qu**, **r**, **s**, **t**, **v**, **w**, **x**, **y**, **z**

- Initial consonant blends: Review: **bl-**, **gl-**, **cl-**, **pl-**, **fl-**, **sl-**, **br-**, **fr-**, **tr-**, **cr-**, **dr-**, **gr-**, **pr-**, **shr-**, **thr-**, **sc-**, **sm-**, **sn-**, **sp-**, **sk-**, **st-**, **squ-**, **sw-**, **tw-**, **dw-**

- Vowel sounds (phonemes): Review: short /a/, short /i/, short /o/, short /e/, short /u/

- Syllabication: Review: Each syllable contains one vowel sound (phoneme).

- Consonant clusters (New): Consonant combinations representing three different consonant phonemes: **str**, **spr**, **spl**, **scr**

Stage 1: Phoneme Production/Replication

Have the students repeat each of these consonant clusters: **str**, **spr**, **spl**, **scr**

Stage 2: Consonant Cluster Isolation

Say **split**. (Repeat **split**.) Say **split**. (Repeat **split**.) What's the cluster in **split**?	(/spl/)
Say **scrap**. (Repeat **scrap**.) Say **scrap**. (Repeat **scrap**.) What's the cluster in **scrap**?	(/scr/)
Say **stress**. (Repeat **stress**.) Say **stress**. (Repeat **stress**.) What's the cluster in **stress**?	(/str/)
Say **sprint**. (Repeat **sprint**.) Say **sprint**. (Repeat **sprint**.) What's the cluster in **sprint**?	(/spr/)
Say **strum**. (Repeat **strum**.) Say **strum**. (Repeat **strum**.) What's the cluster in **strum**?	(/str/)
Say **splendid**. (Repeat **splendid**.) Say **splendid**. (Repeat **splendid**.) What's the cluster in **splendid**?	(/spl/)
Say **scrub**. (Repeat **scrub**.) Say **scrub**. (Repeat **scrub**.) What's the cluster in **scrub**?	(/scr/)

Say **strip**. (Repeat **strip**.) Say **strip**. (Repeat **strip**.) What's the cluster in **strip**?   (/str/)

Say **splash**. (Repeat **splash**.) Say **splash**. (Repeat **splash**.) What's the cluster in **splash**?   (/spl/)

Say **scrimp**. (Repeat **scrimp**.) Say **scrimp**. (Repeat **scrimp**.) What's the cluster in **scrimp**?   (/scr/)

Say **strict**. (Repeat **strict**.) Say **strict**. (Repeat **strict**.) What's the cluster in **strict**?   (/str/)

Say **sprint**. (Repeat **sprint**.) Say **sprint**. (Repeat **sprint**.) What's the cluster in **sprint**?   (/spr/)

Say **splat**. (Repeat **splat**.) Say **splat**. (Repeat **splat**.) What's the cluster in **splat**?   (/spl/)

Say **struck**. (Repeat **struck**.) Say **struck**. (Repeat **struck**.) What's the cluster in **struck**?   (/str/)

Say **scram**. (Repeat **scram**.) Say **scram**. (Repeat **scram**.) What's the cluster in **scram**?   (/scr/)

Stage 3: Phoneme Segmentation and Counting (Spelling the Sounds)

Say **strut**. (Repeat **strut**.) Say **strut**. (Repeat **strut**.) Say the sounds in **strut**.   (/s/ /t/ /r/ /u/ /t/)

Say **split**. (Repeat **split**.) Say **split**. (Repeat **split**.) Say the sounds in **split**.   (/s/ /p/ /l/ /i/ /t/)

Say **scrap**. (Repeat **scrap**.) Say **scrap**. (Repeat **scrap**.) Say the sounds in **scrap**.   (/s/ /k/ /r/ /a/ /p/)

Say **stress**. (Repeat **stress**.) Say **stress**. (Repeat **stress**.) Say the sounds in **stress**.   (/s/ /t/ /r/ /e/ /s/)

Say **stock**. (Repeat **stock**.) Say **stock**. (Repeat **stock**.) Say the sounds in **stock**.   (/s/ /t/ /o/ /k/)

Say **splash**. (Repeat **splash**.) Say **splash**. (Repeat **splash**.) Say the sounds in **splash**.   (/s/ /p/ /l/ /a/ /sh/)

Say **sprung**. (Repeat **sprung**.) Say **sprung**. (Repeat **sprung**.) Say the sounds in **sprung**.   (/s/ /p/ /r/ /u/ /n/ /g/)

Say **swam**. (Repeat **swam**.) Say **swam**. (Repeat **swam**.) Say the sounds in **swam**.   (/s/ /w/ /a/ /m/)

After the students have been introduced to the new unit's vocabulary words, you may ask, "How many sounds in **xxx**?" "How many letters in **xxx**?"

Stage 4: Phoneme Blending

Listen and repeat. Listen and repeat: /s/ /t/ /r/ /a/ /p/. (Repeat phoneme series three times.)   (strap)

Listen and repeat. Listen and repeat: /s/ /k/ /r/ /u/ /b/. (Repeat phoneme series three times.)   (scrub)

Listen and repeat. Listen and repeat: /s/ /p/ /r/ /i/ /g/. (Repeat phoneme series three times.)   (sprig)

Listen and repeat. Listen and repeat: /s/ /t/ /r/ /a/ /n/ /d/. (Repeat phoneme series three times.)   (strand)

Listen and repeat. Listen and repeat: /s/ /t/ /r/ /u/ /m/. (Repeat phoneme series three times.)   (strum)

Listen and repeat. Listen and repeat: /s/ /p/ /l/ /i/ /t/. (Repeat phoneme series three times.)   (split)

Stage 5: Rhyming

Say **strand**. (Repeat **strand**.) Say **strand**. (Repeat **strand**.)
Say a word that rhymes with **strand**.   (band, hand, land)

Say **scram**. (Repeat **scram**.) Say **scram**. (Repeat **scram**.)
Say a word that rhymes with **scram**.   (ham, clam, sham)

Say **strap**. (Repeat **strap**.) Say **strap**. (Repeat **strap**.)
Say a word that rhymes with **strap**.   (map, clap, scrap)

Say **spin**. (Repeat **spin**.) Say **spin**. (Repeat **spin**.)
Say a word that rhymes with **spin**.   (win, din, tin)

Say **stress**. (Repeat **stress**.) Say **stress**. (Repeat **stress**.)
Say a word that rhymes with **stress**.   (dress, less, mess)

Say **cram**. (Repeat **cram**.) Say **cram**. (Repeat **cram**.)
Say a word that rhymes with **cram**.   (clam, ram, swam)

Say **split**. (Repeat **split**.) Say **split**. (Repeat **split**.)
Say a word that rhymes with **split**.   (hit, bit, grit)

Say **strung**. (Repeat **strung**.) Say **strung**. (Repeat **strung**.)
Say a word that rhymes with **strung**.   (hung, sung, lung)

Stage 6: Blend/Cluster Deletion

Say **scrub**. (Repeat **scrub**.) Say **scrub**. (Repeat **scrub**.) Say **scrub** without the */sk/*.   (*/rub/*)

Say **split**. (Repeat **split**.) Say **split**. (Repeat **split**.) Say **split** without the */spl/*.   (*/it/*)

Say **splint**. (Repeat **splint**.) Say **splint**. (Repeat **splint**.) Say **splint** without the */sp/*.   (*/lint/*)

Say **kill**. (Repeat **kill**.) Say **kill**. (Repeat **kill**.) Say **kill** without the */k/*.   (*/ill/*)

Say **strand**. (Repeat **strand**.) Say **strand**. (Repeat **strand**.) Say **strand** without the */str/*.   (*/and/*)

Say **sprig**. (Repeat **sprig**.) Say **sprig**. (Repeat **sprig**.) Say **sprig** without the */sp/*.   (*/rig/*)

Say **plush**. (Repeat **plush**.) Say **plush**. (Repeat **plush**.) Say **plush** without the */p/*.   (*/lush/*)

Say **spin**. (Repeat **spin**.) Say **spin**. (Repeat **spin**.) Say **spin** without the */sp/*.   (*/in/*)

Say **strap**. (Repeat **strap**.) Say **strap**. (Repeat **strap**.) Say **strap** without the */s/*.   (*/trap/*)

Say **scrap**. (Repeat **scrap**.) Say **scrap**. (Repeat **scrap**.) Say **scrap** without the */sc/*.   (*/rap/*)

Say **scram**. (Repeat **scram**.) Say **scram**. (Repeat **scram**.) Say **scram** without the */sk/*.   (*/ram/*)

Say **splash**. (Repeat **splash**.) Say **splash**. (Repeat **splash**.) Say **splash** without the */spl/*.   (*/ash/*)

Stage 7: Phoneme Substitution

Say **cram**. (Repeat **cram**.) Say **cram**. (Repeat **cram**.) Now, change the first sound in **cram** to /p/. (pram)

Say **shell**. (Repeat **shell**.) Say **shell**. (Repeat **shell**.) Now, change the first sound in **shell** to /b/. (bell)

Say **fling**. (Repeat **fling**.) Say **fling**. (Repeat **fling**.) Now, change the first sound in **fling** to /s/. (sling)

Say **slug**. (Repeat **slug**.) Say **slug**. (Repeat **slug**.) Now, change the first sound in **slug** to /p/. (plug)

Say **crumb**. (Repeat **crumb**.) Say **crumb**. (Repeat **crumb**.) Now, change the first sound in **crumb** to /d/. (drum)

Say **clunk**. (Repeat **clunk**.) Say **clunk**. (Repeat **clunk**.) Now, change the first sound in **clunk** to /p/. (plunk)

Advancement: Substitute isolated phonemes and blends for initial consonant clusters:

Say **string**. (Repeat **string**.) Say **string**. (Repeat **string**.) Now, change the /str/ to /d/. (ding)

Say **struck**. (Repeat **struck**.) Say **struck**. (Repeat **struck**.) Now, change the /str/ to /l/. (luck)

Say **spring**. (Repeat **spring**.) Say **spring**. (Repeat **spring**.) Now, change the /spr/ to /th/. (thing)

Say **scrap**. (Repeat **scrap**.) Say **scrap**. (Repeat **scrap**.) Now, change the /scr/ to /t/. (tap)

Say **strand**. (Repeat **strand**.) Say **strand**. (Repeat **strand**.) Now, change the /str/ to /s/. (sand)

Say **splash**. (Repeat **splash**.) Say **splash**. (Repeat **splash**.) Now, change the /spl/ to /k/. (cash)

Say **strip**. (Repeat **strip**.) Say **strip**. (Repeat **strip**.) Now, change the /str/ to /ch/. (chip)

Stage 8: Phoneme Reversal

Say **ten**. (Repeat **ten**.) Say **ten**. (Repeat **ten**.)
Now, change the first sound to last, and the last sound to first. (net)

Say **tap**. (Repeat **tap**.) Say **tap**. (Repeat **tap**.)
Now, change the first sound to last, and the last sound to first. (pat)

Say **dock**. (Repeat **dock**.) Say **dock**. (Repeat **dock**.)
Now, change the first sound to last, and the last sound to first. (cod)

Say **tell**. (Repeat **tell**.) Say **tell**. (Repeat **tell**.)
Now, change the first sound to last, and the last sound to first. (let)

Say **tub**. (Repeat **tub**.) Say **tub**. (Repeat **tub**.)
Now, change the first sound to last, and the last sound to first. (but)

Say **sub**. (Repeat **sub**.) Say **sub**. (Repeat **sub**.)
Now, change the first sound to last, and the last sound to first. (bus)

Say **gas**. (Repeat **gas**.) Say **gas**. (Repeat **gas**.)
Now, change the first sound to last, and the last sound to first.   (sag)

Stage 9: Pig Latin

Three or four modelings may be necessary with this activity, particularly for students with a significant lack of phonemic awareness. Do not penalize students who cannot master Pig Latin.

Say **string**. (Repeat **string**.) Say **string**. (Repeat **string**.) Say **string** without the */str/*.   (*/ing/*)

Say */ing/*. (Repeat */ing/*.) Say */ing/*. (Repeat */ing/*.) Say */ing/* with */str/* at the end.   (*/ing str/*)

Now, add */ay/* at the end.   (*/ing stray/*)

Say **splash**. (Repeat **splash**.) Say **splash**. (Repeat **splash**.) Say **splash** without the */spl/*.   (*/ash/*)

Say */ash/*. (Repeat */ash/*.) Say */ash/*. (Repeat */ash/*.) Say */ash/* with */spl/* at the end.   (*/ash spl/*)

Now, add */ay/* at the end.   (*/ash splay/*)

Say **sprocket**. (Repeat **sprocket**.) Say **sprocket**. (Repeat **sprocket**.)
Say **sprocket** without the */spr/*.   (*/ock et/*)

Say */ocket/*. (Repeat */ocket/*.) Say */ocket/*. (Repeat */ocket/*.) Say */ocket/* with */spr/*
at the end.   (*/ock et spr/*)

Now, add */ay/* at the end.   (*/ock et spray/*)

Say **stranded**. (Repeat **stranded**.) Say **stranded**. (Repeat **stranded**.)
Say **stranded** without the */str/*.   (*/and ed/*)

Say */anded/*. (Repeat */anded/*.) Say */anded/*. (Repeat */anded/*.) Say */anded/* with
/str/ at the end.   (*/and ed str/*)

Now, add */ay/* at the end.   (*/and ed stray/*)

Now, say together in Pig Latin: "I can speak Pig Latin."   (Iay ancay eakspay igpay atinlay)

Suggestions for Related Activities

Create possible double-syllable and multisyllable English words. Have the students work individually or in groups, using:

- The four previously mastered short vowels: <u>**a**</u>, <u>**e**</u>, <u>**i**</u>, and <u>**o**</u>

- All of the consonant letters

- Previously mastered spelling rules: <u>**-ck**</u> for */k/*; <u>**qu**</u> for */kw/*; <u>**x**</u> for */ks/*; <u>**s**</u> for */z/*; and doubling <u>**-ll**</u>, <u>**-ff**</u>, <u>**-ss**</u>, and <u>**-zz**</u> after short vowels at the ends of words

- Consonant digraphs <u>**ch**</u>, <u>**th**</u>, <u>**sh**</u>, and <u>**wh**</u>

- Initial consonant blends
- Consonant clusters

Reading/Spelling Vocabulary

Scott	sprang	stress	strum
scram	spring	strict	strung
scraps	sprung	string	*were*
splash	strap	strip	
split	street	strong	

Unit 17

Phonemic Awareness Drills

These sequential, cumulative drills assess and build phoneme awareness in emerging readers and spellers. To initiate daily lessons, present portions of these drills orally—without corresponding letters. Phonemes (sounds) should be mastered before they are associated with their orthographic representations (letters). After phonemic awareness has been established for a unit's new phonology concepts, students can be introduced to the unit's new symbol-sound correspondences and its reading/spelling vocabulary.

Phonology Concepts for Unit 17

- Consonant sounds (phonemes): Review: /b/, /d/, /f/, /g/, /h/, /j/, /k/, /l/, /m/, /n/, /p/, /r/, /s/, /t/, /v/, /w/, /y/, /z/

- Consonant letters (graphemes): Review: **b**, **c**, **d**, **f**, **g**, **h**, **j**, **k**, **l**, **m**, **n**, **p**, **qu**, **r**, **s**, **t**, **v**, **w**, **x**, **y**, **z**

- Initial consonant blends: Review: **bl-**, **gl-**, **cl-**, **pl-**, **fl-**, **sl-**, **br-**, **fr-**, **tr-**, **cr-**, **dr-**, **gr-**, **pr-**, **shr-**, **thr-**, **sc-**, **sm-**, **sn-**, **sp-**, **sk-**, **st-**, **squ-**, **sw-**, **tw-**, **dw-**

- Vowel sounds (phonemes): Review: short /a/, short /i/, short /o/, short /e/, short /u/

- Syllabication: Review: Each syllable contains one vowel sound (phoneme).

- Consonant clusters: Review: **str**, **spr**, **spl**, **scr**

- Final consonant blends: New: Final blends represent two different consonant phonemes at ends of words: **-st**, **-sk**, **-sp**, **-mp**, **-nd**, **-ld**, **-lk**, **-lp**, **-lt**, **-ft**, **-nt**, **-pt**, **-ct**

Stage 1: Phoneme Production/Replication

Have the students repeat each final blend: /st/, /sk/, /sp/, /mp/, /nd/, /ld/, /lk/, /lp/, /lt/, /ft/, /nt/, /pt/, /kt/. Provide examples of words ending with each blend. (For examples, refer to the reading/spelling vocabulary list for Unit 17.)

Stage 2: Phoneme Isolation

Say **fast**. (Repeat **fast**.) Say **fast**. (Repeat **fast**.) What's the last blend in **fast**?   (/st/)

Say **dusk**. (Repeat **dusk**.) Say **dusk**. (Repeat **dusk**.) What's the last blend in **dusk**?   (/sk/)

Say **bend**. (Repeat **bend**.) Say **bend**. (Repeat **bend**.) What's the last blend in **bend**? (/nd/)

Say **bump**. (Repeat **bump**.) Say **bump**. (Repeat **bump**.) What's the last blend in **bump**?   (/mp/)

Say **weld**. (Repeat **weld**.) Say **weld**. (Repeat **weld**.) What's the last blend in **weld**? (/ld/)

Say **contrast**. (Repeat **contrast**.) Say **contrast**. (Repeat **contrast**.)
What's the last blend in **contrast**?   (/st/)

Say **bulk**. (Repeat **bulk**.) Say **bulk**. (Repeat **bulk**.) What's the last blend in **bulk**? (/lk/)

Say **melt**. (Repeat **melt**.) Say **melt**. (Repeat **melt**.) What's the last blend in **melt**? (/lt/)

Say **comment**. (Repeat **comment**.) Say **comment**. (Repeat **comment**.)
What's the last blend in **comment**?   (/nt/)

Say **conduct**. (Repeat **conduct**.) Say **conduct**. (Repeat **conduct**.)
What's the last blend in **conduct**?   (/kt/)

Stage 3: Phoneme Segmentation and Counting (Spelling the Sounds)

Say **flint**. (Repeat **flint**.) Say **flint**. (Repeat **flint**.) Say the sounds in **flint**.   (/f/ /l/ /i/ /n/ /t/)

Say **champ**. (Repeat **champ**.) Say **champ**. (Repeat **champ**.) Say the sounds
in **champ**.   (/ch/ /a/ /m/ /p/)

Say **strand**. (Repeat **strand**.) Say **strand**. (Repeat **strand**.) Say the sounds in **strand**. (/s/ /t/ /r/ /a/ /n/ /d/)

Say **stock**. (Repeat **stock**.) Say **stock**. (Repeat **stock**.) Say the sounds in **stock**.   (/s/ /t/ /o/ /k/)

Say **splash**. (Repeat **splash**.) Say **splash**. (Repeat **splash**.) Say the sounds in **splash**. (/s/ /p/ /l/ /a/ /sh/)

Say **sprung**. (Repeat **sprung**.) Say **sprung**. (Repeat **sprung**.) Say the sounds
in **sprung**.   (/s/ /p/ /r/ /u/ /n/ /g/)

Say **swam**. (Repeat **swam**.) Say **swam**. (Repeat **swam**.) Say the sounds in **swam**.   (/s/ /w/ /a/ /m/)

After the students have been introduced to the new unit's vocabulary words, you may ask, "How many sounds in **xxx**?" "How many letters in **xxx**?"

Stage 4: Phoneme Blending

Listen and repeat. Listen and repeat: /s/ /t/ /r/ /a/ /p/. (Repeat phoneme series three times.)   (strap)

Listen and repeat. Listen and repeat: /s/ /k/ /r/ /u/ /b/. (Repeat phoneme series three times.)   (scrub)

Listen and repeat. Listen and repeat: /s/ /p/ /r/ /i/ /g/. (Repeat phoneme series three times.)   (sprig)

Listen and repeat. Listen and repeat: /s/ /t/ /r/ /a/ /n/ /d/. (Repeat phoneme series three times.)   (strand)

Listen and repeat. Listen and repeat: /s/ /t/ /r/ /u/ /m/. (Repeat phoneme series three times.)   (strum)

Listen and repeat. Listen and repeat: /s/ /p/ /l/ /i/ /t/. (Repeat phoneme series three times.)   (split)

Stage 5: Rhyming

Say **thump**. (Repeat **thump**.) Say **thump**. (Repeat **thump**.)
Say a word that rhymes with **thump**.   (bump, lump, clump)

Say **plant**. (Repeat **plant**.) Say **plant**. (Repeat **plant**.)
Say a word that rhymes with **plant**.   (ant, grant, pant)

Say **vent**. (Repeat **vent**.) Say **vent**. (Repeat **vent**.)
Say a word that rhymes with **vent**.   (lent, sent, went)

Say **primp**. (Repeat **primp**.) Say **primp**. (Repeat **primp**.)
Say a word that rhymes with **primp**.   (imp, skimp, limp)

Say **blend**. (Repeat **blend**.) Say **blend**. (Repeat **blend**.)
Say a word that rhymes with **blend**.   (bend, lend, mend)

Say **quilt**. (Repeat **quilt**.) Say **quilt**. (Repeat **quilt**.)
Say a word that rhymes with **quilt**.   (stilt, kilt, tilt)

Say **split**. (Repeat **split**.) Say **split**. (Repeat **split**.)
Say a word that rhymes with **split**.   (hit, bit, grit)

Say **strung**. (Repeat **strung**.) Say **strung**. (Repeat **strung**.)
Say a word that rhymes with **strung**.   (hung, sung, lung)

Stage 6: Cluster/Blend Deletion

Say **mend**. (Repeat **mend**.) Say **mend**. (Repeat **mend**.) Say **mend** without the /d/.   (/men/)

Say **fund**. (Repeat **fund**.) Say **fund**. (Repeat **fund**.) Say **fund** without the /d/.   (/fun/)

Say **silt**. (Repeat **silt**.) Say **silt**. (Repeat **silt**.) Say **silt** without the /t/.   (/sill/)

Say **clump**. (Repeat **clump**.) Say **clump**. (Repeat **clump**.) Say **clump** without the /k/.   (/lump/)

Say **strand**. (Repeat **strand**.) Say **strand**. (Repeat **strand**.) Say **strand** without
the /str/.   (/and/)

Say **mend**. (Repeat **mend**.) Say **mend**. (Repeat **mend**.) Say **mend** without the /m/.   (/end/)

Say **plush**. (Repeat **plush**.) Say **plush**. (Repeat **plush**.) Say **plush** without the /p/.   (/lush/)

Say **ramp**. (Repeat **ramp**.) Say **ramp**. (Repeat **ramp**.) Say **ramp** without the /r/.   (/amp/)

Say **plant**. (Repeat **plant**.) Say **plant**. (Repeat **plant**.) Say **plant** without the /t/.   (/plan/)

Say **scrap**. (Repeat **scrap**.) Say **scrap**. (Repeat **scrap**.) Say **scrap** without the /sc/.   (/rap/)

Say **tend**. (Repeat **tend**.) Say **tend**. (Repeat **tend**.) Say **tend** without the /d/.   (/ten/)

Say **fund**. (Repeat **fund**.) Say **fund**. (Repeat **fund**.) Say **fund** without the /d/.   (/fun/)

Stage 7: Phoneme Substitution

Say **tend**. (Repeat **tend**.) Say **tend**. (Repeat **tend**.) Now, change the first sound in **tend** to /s/.   (send)

Say **think**. (Repeat **think**.) Say **think**. (Repeat **think**.) Now, change the first sound in **think** to /m/.   (mink)

Say **lend**. (Repeat **lend**.) Say **lend**. (Repeat **lend**.) Now, change the first sound in **lend** to /t/.   (tend)

Say **help**. (Repeat **help**.) Say **help**. (Repeat **help**.) Now, change the first sound in **help** to /y/.   (yelp)

Say **milk**. (Repeat **milk**.) Say **milk**. (Repeat **milk**.) Now, change the first sound in **milk** to /s/.   (silk)

Say **craft**. (Repeat **craft**.) Say **craft**. (Repeat **craft**.) Now, change the first sound in **craft** to /d/.   (draft)

Advancement: After initial phoneme(s), substitute final phoneme(s):

Say **wins**. (Repeat **wins**.) Say **wins**. (Repeat **wins**.) Now, change the last sound in **wins** to /d/.   (wind)

Say **fizz**. (Repeat **fizz**.) Say **fizz**. (Repeat **fizz**.) Now, change the last sound in **fizz** to /n/.   (fin)

Say **meld**. (Repeat **meld**.) Say **meld**. (Repeat **meld**.) Now, change the last sound in **meld** to /t/.   (melt)

Say **spent**. (Repeat **spent**.) Say **spent**. (Repeat **spent**.) Now, change the last sound in **spent** to /d/.   (spend)

Say **plum**. (Repeat **plum**.) Say **plum**. (Repeat **plum**.) Now, change the last sound in **plum** to /g/.   (plug)

Say **bend**. (Repeat **bend**.) Say **bend**. (Repeat **bend**.) Now, change the last sound in **bend** to /ch/.   (bench)

Say **cast**. (Repeat **cast**.) Say **cast**. (Repeat **cast**.) Now, change the last sound in **cast** to /k/.   (cask)

Say **lisp**. (Repeat **lisp**.) Say **lisp**. (Repeat **lisp**.) Now, change the last sound in **lisp** to /t/.   (list)

Stage 8: Phoneme Reversal

Say **pan**. (Repeat **pan**.) Say **pan**. (Repeat **pan**.)
Now, change the first sound to last, and the last sound to first.   (nap)

Say **sell**. (Repeat **sell**.) Say **sell**. (Repeat **sell**.)
Now, change the first sound to last, and the last sound to first.   (less)

Say **ten**. (Repeat **ten**.) Say **ten**. (Repeat **ten**.)
Now, change the first sound to last, and the last sound to first.   (net)

Say **sick**. (Repeat **sick**.) Say **sick**. (Repeat **sick**.)
Now, change the first sound to last, and the last sound to first.   (kiss)

Say **pill**. (Repeat **pill**.) Say **pill**. (Repeat **pill**.)
Now, change the first sound to last, and the last sound to first.   (lip)

Say **back**. (Repeat **back**.) Say **back**. (Repeat **back**.)
Now, change the first sound to last, and the last sound to first.   (cab)

Say **much**. (Repeat **much**.) Say **much**. (Repeat **much**.)
Now, change the first sound to last, and the last sound to first.   (chum)

Stage 9: Pig Latin

Three or four modelings may be necessary with this activity, particularly for students with a significant lack of phonemic awareness. Do not penalize students who cannot master Pig Latin.

Say **scrimp**. (Repeat **scrimp**.) Say **scrimp**. (Repeat **scrimp**.) Say **scrimp**
without the */scr/*.   (*/imp/*)

Say */imp/*. (Repeat */imp/*.) Say */imp/*. (Repeat */imp/*.) Say */imp/* with */scr/* at the end. (*/imp scr/*)

Now, say */ay/* at the end.   (*/imp scray/*)

Say **pants**. (Repeat **pants**.) Say **pants**. (Repeat **pants**.) Say **pants** without the */p/*.   (*/ants/*)

Say */ants/*. (Repeat */ants/*.) Say */ants/*. (Repeat */ants/*.) Say */ants/* with */p/* at the end. (*/ants p/*)

Now, say */ay/* at the end.   (*/ants pay/*)

Say **strand**. (Repeat **strand**.) Say **strand**. (Repeat **strand**.) Say **strand** without the */str/*. (*/and/*)

Say */and/*. (Repeat */and/*.) Say */and/*. (Repeat */and/*.) Say */and/* with */str/* at the end. (*/and str/*)

Now, say */ay/* at the end.   (*/and stray/*)

Say **chunk**. (Repeat **chunk**.) Say **chunk**. (Repeat **chunk**.)
Now, say **chunk** without the */ch/*.   (*/unk/*)

Say */unk/*. (Repeat */unk/*.) Say */unk/*. (Repeat */unk/*.)
Say */unk/* with */ch/* at the end.   (*/unk ch/*)

Now, say */ay/* at the end.   (*/unk chay/*)

Now, say together in Pig Latin: "I can speak Pig Latin."   (Iay ancay eakspay igpay atinlay)

Suggestions for Related Activities

- Create possible double-syllable and multisyllable English words. Have the students work individually or in groups, using:

  – The four previously mastered short vowels: **a**, **e**, **i**, and **o**

  – All of the consonant letters

  – Previously mastered spelling rules: **-ck** for */k/*; **qu** for */kw/*; **x** for */ks/*; **s** for */z/*; and doubling **-ll**, **-ff**, **-ss**, and **-zz** after short vowels at the ends of words

- Consonant digraphs <u>ch</u>, <u>th</u>, <u>sh</u>, and <u>wh</u>

- Initial consonant blends

- Consonant clusters

• Present some morphologic awareness activities:

- Supply a root such as **port** or **form**, with several potential prefixes and suffixes. Ask the students to (orally) create as many possible English words as they can from these roots, prefixes, and suffixes.

• Present some syntactic awareness activities:

- Supply some simple sentences and have students supply a "how," then a "when," then a "where"—thereby introducing the procedure for sentence expansion in English.

- Say "The teachers park in this lot." Now, change the sentence to a question. (Do the teachers park in this lot?)

Reading/Spelling Vocabulary

act	dent	kilt	silk	trust
ask	drift	last	soft	*any*
best	dusk	mask	start	*do*
blond	frost	mint	stump	*many*
clumps	grand	pump	Trick 'r Treat	*two*

Unit 18

Phonemic Awareness Drills

These sequential, cumulative drills assess and build phonemic awareness in emerging readers and spellers. To initiate daily lessons, present portions of these drills orally—without corresponding letters. Phonemes (sounds) should be mastered before they are associated with their orthographic representations (letters). After phonemic awareness has been established for a unit's new phonology concepts, students can be introduced to the unit's new symbol-sound correspondences and its reading/spelling vocabulary.

Phonology Concepts for Unit 18

- Consonant sounds (phonemes): Review: /b/, /d/, /f/, /g/, /h/, /j/, /k/, /l/, /m/, /n/, /p/, /r/, /s/, /t/, /v/, /w/, /y/, /z/

- Consonant letters (graphemes): Review: **b**, **c**, **d**, **f**, g, **h**, j, **k**, **l**, **m**, **n**, **p**, **qu**, **r**, **s**, **t**, **v**, **w**, **x**, **y**, **z**

- Initial consonant blends: Review: **bl-**, **gl-**, **cl-**, **pl-**, **fl-**, **sl-**, **br-**, **fr-**, **tr-**, **cr-**, **dr-**, **gr-**, **pr-**, **shr-**, **thr-**, **sc-**, **sm-**, **sn-**, **sp-**, **sk-**, **st-**, **squ-**, **sw-**, **tw-**, **dw-**

- Vowel sounds (phonemes): Review: short /a/, short /i/, short /o/, short /e/, short /u/

- Syllabication: Review: Each syllable contains one vowel sound (phoneme).

- Consonant clusters: Review: **str**, **spr**, **spl**, **scr**

- Final consonant blends: Review: **-st**, **-sk**, **-sp**, **-mp**, **-nd**, **-ld**, **-lk**, **-lp**, **-lt**, **-ft**, **-nt**, **-pt**, **-ct**

- Spelling /ch/ as **-tch**: New: The phoneme /ch/ is usually spelled **-tch** after short vowels at the ends of one-syllable words. Examples: crutch, latch, notch, pitch, hatch, witch. Exceptions: such, rich, much, which.

Stage 1: Phoneme Production/Replication

Have the students repeat this consonant phoneme: /ch/.

- Ask the students: In spelling, what silent letter usually comes before **-ch** at the ends of single-syllable words?   **t**

- Ask the students: Which four vocabulary words are not spelled with final **-tch**?   **such**, **rich**, **much**, **which**

Display, and have the students repeat, this mnemonic: Such rich people have much which they can spend.

Stage 2: Phoneme Isolation

Say **check**. (Repeat **check**.) Say **check**. (Repeat **check**.)
What's the first sound in **check**?　　　　　　　　　　　　　　　*(/ch/)*

Say **hatch**. (Repeat **hatch**.) Say **hatch**. (Repeat **hatch**.)
What's the last sound in **hatch**?　　　　　　　　　　　　　　　*(/ch/)*

Say **hatch**. (Repeat **hatch**.) Say **hatch**. (Repeat **hatch**.)
What's the vowel sound in **hatch**?　　　　　　　　　　　*(/a/) (short **a**)*

Say **shop**. (Repeat **shop**.) Say **shop**. (Repeat **shop**.)
What's the first sound in **shop**?　　　　　　　　　　　　　　　*(/sh/)*

Say **notch**. (Repeat **notch**.) Say **notch**. (Repeat **notch**.)
What's the last sound in **notch**?　　　　　　　　　　　　　　　*(/ch/)*

Say **much**. (Repeat **much**.) Say **much**. (Repeat **much**.)
What's the vowel sound in **much**?　　　　　　　　　　　*(/u/) (short **u**)*

Say **fetch**. (Repeat **fetch**.) Say **fetch**. (Repeat **fetch**.)
What's the vowel sound in **fetch**?　　　　　　　　　　　*(/e/) (short **e**)*

Say **sketch**. (Repeat **sketch**.) Say **sketch**. (Repeat **sketch**.)
What's the last sound in **sketch**?　　　　　　　　　　　　　　　*(/ch/)*

Say **weld**. (Repeat **weld**.) Say **weld**. (Repeat **weld**.)
What's the first sound in **weld**?　　　　　　　　　　　　　　　*(/w/)*

Say **stitch**. (Repeat **stitch**.) Say **stitch**. (Repeat **stitch**.)
What's the vowel sound in **stitch**?　　　　　　　　　　　*(/i/) (short **i**)*

Say **witch**. (Repeat **witch**.) Say **witch**. (Repeat **witch**.)
What's the first sound in **witch**?　　　　　　　　　　　　　　　*(/w/)*

Say **botch**. (Repeat **botch**.) Say **botch**. (Repeat **botch**.)
What's the vowel sound in **botch**?　　　　　　　　　　　*(/o/) (short **o**)*

Say **glitch**. (Repeat **glitch**.) Say **glitch**. (Repeat **glitch**.)
What's the last sound in **glitch**?　　　　　　　　　　　　　　　*(/ch/)*

Stage 3: Phoneme Segmentation and Counting (Spelling the Sounds)

Say **match**. (Repeat **match**.) Say **match**. (Repeat **match**.)
Say the sounds in **match**.　　　　　　　　　　　　*(/m/ /a/ /ch/)*

Say **stretch**. (Repeat **stretch**.) Say **stretch**. (Repeat **stretch**.)
Say the sounds in **stretch**.　　　　　　　　　*(/s/ /t/ /r/ /e/ /ch/)*

Say **twitch**. (Repeat **twitch**.) Say **twitch**. (Repeat **twitch**.)
Say the sounds in **twitch**.　　　　　　　　　　*(/t/ /w/ /i/ /ch/)*

Say **fetch**. (Repeat **fetch**.) Say **fetch**. (Repeat **fetch**.) Say the sounds in **fetch**.   (/f/ /e/ /ch/)

Say **catch**. (Repeat **catch**.) Say **catch**. (Repeat **catch**.) Say the sounds in **catch**.   (/c/ /a/ /ch/)

Say **sketch**. (Repeat **sketch**.) Say **sketch**. (Repeat **sketch**.) Say the sounds in **sketch**.   (/s/ /k/ /e/ /ch/)

Say **pitch**. (Repeat **pitch**.) Say **pitch**. (Repeat **pitch**.) Say the sounds in **pitch**.   (/p/ /i/ /ch/)

After the students have been introduced to the new unit's vocabulary words, you may ask, "How many sounds in **xxx**?" "How many letters in **xxx**?"

Stage 4: Phoneme Blending

Listen and repeat. Listen and repeat: /s/ /k/ /r/ /a/ /ch/.
(Repeat phoneme series three times.)   (scratch)

Listen and repeat. Listen and repeat: /k/ /l/ /u/ /ch/.
(Repeat phoneme series three times.)   (clutch)

Listen and repeat. Listen and repeat: /t/ /w/ /i/ /ch/.
(Repeat phoneme series three times.)   (twitch)

Listen and repeat. Listen and repeat: /s/ /t/ /r/ /e/ /ch/.
(Repeat phoneme series three times.)   (stretch)

Listen and repeat. Listen and repeat: /th/ /a/ /ch/.
(Repeat phoneme series three times.)   (thatch)

Listen and repeat. Listen and repeat: /p/ /a/ /ch/.
(Repeat phoneme series three times.)   (patch)

Stage 5: Rhyming

Say **match**. (Repeat **match**.) Say **match**. (Repeat **match**.)
Say a word that rhymes with **match**.   (latch, hatch, catch)

Say **etch**. (Repeat **etch**.) Say **etch**. (Repeat **etch**.)
Say a word that rhymes with **etch**.   (sketch, fetch, stretch)

Say **vent**. (Repeat **vent**.) Say **vent**. (Repeat **vent**.)
Say a word that rhymes with **vent**.   (lent, bent, sent)

Say **much**. (Repeat **much**.) Say **much**. (Repeat **much**.)
Say a word that rhymes with **much**.   (hutch, touch, such)

Say **blend**. (Repeat **blend**.) Say **blend**. (Repeat **blend**.)
Say a word that rhymes with **blend**.   (bend, lend, mend)

Say **quilt**. (Repeat **quilt**.) Say **quilt**. (Repeat **quilt**.)
Say a word that rhymes with **quilt**.   (stilt, kilt, tilt)

Say **itch**. (Repeat **itch**.) Say **itch**. (Repeat **itch**.)
Say a word that rhymes with **itch**.   (pitch, hitch, stitch)

Say **notch**. (Repeat **notch**.) Say **notch**. (Repeat **notch**.)
Say a word that rhymes with **notch**.   (botch, watch, blotch)

Stage 6: Phoneme Deletion

Say **fetch**. (Repeat **fetch**.) Say **fetch**. (Repeat **fetch**.) Say **fetch** without the /f/.   (/etch/)

Say **twitch**. (Repeat **twitch**.) Say **twitch**. (Repeat **twitch**.) Say **twitch** without the /t/.   (/witch/)

Say **spark**. (Repeat **spark**.) Say **spark**. (Repeat **spark**.) Say **spark** without the /k/.   (/spar/)

Say **blotch**. (Repeat **blotch**.) Say **blotch**. (Repeat **blotch**.) Say **blotch** without the /l/.   (/botch/)

Say **strand**. (Repeat **strand**.) Say **strand**. (Repeat **strand**.) Say **strand** without the /str/.   (/and/)

Say **mend**. (Repeat **mend**.) Say **mend**. (Repeat **mend**.) Say **mend** without the /m/.   (/end/)

Say **plush**. (Repeat **plush**.) Say **plush**. (Repeat **plush**.) Say **plush** without the /p/.   (/lush/)

Say **pitch**. (Repeat **pitch**.) Say **pitch**. (Repeat **pitch**.) Say **pitch** without the /p/.   (/itch/)

Say **which**. (Repeat **which**.) Say **which**. (Repeat **which**.) Say **which** without the /wh/.   (/itch/)

Say **scrap**. (Repeat **scrap**.) Say **scrap**. (Repeat **scrap**.) Say **scrap** without the /sc/.   (/rap/)

Say **crash**. (Repeat **crash**.) Say **crash**. (Repeat **crash**.) Say **crash** without the /k/.   (/rash/)

Say **stretch**. (Repeat **stretch**.) Say **stretch**. (Repeat **stretch**.) Say **stretch** without the /st/.   (/retch/)

Stage 7: Phoneme Substitution

Say **which**. (Repeat **which**.) Say **which**. (Repeat **which**.)
Now, change the first sound in **which** to /d/.   (ditch)

Say **such**. (Repeat **such**.) Say **such**. (Repeat **such**.)
Now, change the first sound in **such** to /m/.   (much)

Say **thick**. (Repeat **thick**.) Say **thick**. (Repeat **thick**.)
Now, change the first sound in **thick** to /ch/.   (chick)

Say **well**. (Repeat **well**.) Say **well**. (Repeat **well**.)
Now, change the first sound in **well** to /y/.   (yell)

Say **rich**. (Repeat **rich**.) Say **rich**. (Repeat **rich**.)
Now, change the first sound in **rich** to /w/.   (witch)

Say **latch**. (Repeat **latch**.) Say **latch**. (Repeat **latch**.)
Now, change the first sound in **latch** to /b/.   (batch)

Advancement: After initial phoneme(s), substitute medial phoneme(s) and final phoneme(s):

Say **rich**. (Repeat **rich**.) Say **rich**. (Repeat **rich**.)
Now, change the last sound in **rich** to /*b*/.   (rib)

Say **sketch**. (Repeat **sketch**.) Say **sketch**. (Repeat **sketch**.)
Now, change the vowel sound in **sketch** to /*o*/.   (scotch)

Say **chap**. (Repeat **chap**.) Say **chap**. (Repeat **chap**.)
Now, change the last sound in **chap** to /*t*/.   (chat)

Say **botch**. (Repeat **botch**.) Say **botch**. (Repeat **botch**.)
Now, change the vowel sound in **botch** to /*a*/.   (batch)

Say **ditch**. (Repeat **ditch**.) Say **ditch**. (Repeat **ditch**.)
Now, change the first sound in **ditch** to /*wh*/.   (which)

Say **batch**. (Repeat **batch**.) Say **batch**. (Repeat **batch**.)
Now, change the last sound in **batch** to /*k*/.   (back)

Say **hitch**. (Repeat **hitch**.) Say **hitch**. (Repeat **hitch**.)
Now, change the vowel sound in **hitch** to /*u*/.   (hutch)

Say **hutch**. (Repeat **hutch**.) Say **hutch**. (Repeat **hutch**.)
Now, change the last sound in **hutch** to /*m*/.   (hum)

Say **patch**. (Repeat **patch**.) Say **patch**. (Repeat **patch**.)
Now, change the vowel sound in **patch** to /*i*/.   (pitch)

Stage 8: Phoneme Reversal

Say **chip**. (Repeat **chip**.) Say **chip**. (Repeat **chip**.)
Now, change the first sound to last, and the last sound to first.   (pitch)

Say **chap**. (Repeat **chap**.) Say **chap**. (Repeat **chap**.)
Now, change the first sound to last, and the last sound to first.   (patch)

Say **dock**. (Repeat **dock**.) Say **dock**. (Repeat **dock**.)
Now, change the first sound to last, and the last sound to first.   (cod)

Say **much**. (Repeat **much**.) Say **much**. (Repeat **much**.)
Now, change the first sound to last, and the last sound to first.   (chum)

Say **cash**. (Repeat **cash**.) Say **cash**. (Repeat **cash**.)
Now, change the first sound to last, and the last sound to first.   (shack)

Stage 9: Pig Latin

Three or four modelings may be necessary with this activity, particularly for students with a significant lack of phonemic awareness. Do not penalize students who cannot master Pig Latin.

Say **sketch**. (Repeat **sketch**.) Say **sketch**. (Repeat **sketch**.) Say **sketch** without the */sk/*.	*(/etch/)*
Say */etch/*. (Repeat */etch/*.) Say */etch/*. (Repeat */etch/*.) Say */etch/* with */sk/* at the end.	*(/etch sk/)*
Now, add */ay/* at the end.	*(/etch skay/)*
Say **ditch**. (Repeat **ditch**.) Say **ditch**. (Repeat **ditch**.) Say **ditch** without the */d/*.	*(/itch/)*
Say */itch/*. (Repeat */itch/*.) Say */itch/*. (Repeat */itch/*.) Say */itch/* with */d/* at the end.	*(/itch d/)*
Now, add */ay/* at the end.	*(/itch day/)*
Say **crutch**. (Repeat **crutch**.) Say **crutch**. (Repeat **crutch**.) Say **crutch** without the */cr/*.	*(/utch/)*
Say */utch/*. (Repeat */utch/*.) Say */utch/*. (Repeat */utch/*.) Say */utch/* with */cr/* at the end.	*(/utch cr/)*
Now, add */ay/* at the end.	*(/utch cray/)*
Now, say together in Pig Latin: "I can speak Pig Latin."	(Iay ancay eakspay igpay atinlay)

Advancement

All five short vowels; closed syllables; initial and final consonant blends; and consonant clusters have been mastered, along with several spelling rules. With a solid foundation of phonemic awareness skills in place, the students should be ready to move on to Levels 2 and 3 of the *LANGUAGE !* curriculum. Beginning with Unit 19, syllable types and their inherent vowel differences (**-r** control, open syllables, final silent **-e**, vowel digraphs, diphthongs, and final stable syllable **c** + **-le**) are sequentially and cumulatively mastered. Contextual analysis and critical reading are also emphasized in Level 2.

In Levels 2 and 3, morphemes from Anglo-Saxon, Latin, and Greek are introduced. The grammar of English is taught sequentially and cumulatively, integrated and woven through a structured composition strand. The curriculum also continues to emphasize reading comprehension of narrative and expository text, through all of the levels of Bloom's *Taxonomy*. All fifteen language arts strands develop in Levels 2 and 3. Level 3 also introduces and provides for mastery of more advanced principles of grammar, composition, and literature.

Reading/Spelling Vocabulary

batch	fetch	kitchen	patch	stretch
catch	hatch	latch	pitch	switch
clutch	hutch	match	sketch	watch
ditch	itching	notch	stitch	

References

Adams, M. (1990). *Beginning to read: Learning and thinking about print.* Cambridge, MA: MIT Press.

Adams, M. & Bruck, M. (1995). Resolving the 'great debate.' *American Educator*, 19.

Beck, I. & Juel, C. (1995). The role of decoding in learning to read. *American Educator*, 19.

Blachman, B. (1994). Early literacy acquisition: The role of phonological awareness. In G.P. Wallach and K.G. Butler (Eds.), *Language learning disabilities in school-age children and adolescents.* New York: Merrill.

Brady, S., Fowler, A., Stone, B., & Winbury, N. (1994). Training phonological awareness: An inner-city intervention project. *Annals of Dyslexia, 44.*

Brady, S. & Shankweiler, D. (Eds.). (1991). *Phonological processes in literacy: A tribute to Isabelle Y. Liberman.* Hillsdale, NJ: Lawrence Erlbaum Associates.

Byrne, B. & Fielding-Barnsley, R. (1995). Evaluation of a program to teach phonemic awareness to young children: A 2- and 3-year follow-up and a new preschool trial. *Journal of Educational Psychology, 85.*

Cunningham, A.E. (1990). Explicit versus implicit instruction in phonemic awareness. *Journal of Experimental Child Psychology, 50.*

Felton, R. (1993). Effects of instruction on the decoding skills of children with phonological processing problems. *Journal of Learning Disabilities, 26.*

Foorman, B.R., Francis, D.J., Beeler, T., Winikates, D., & Fletcher, J.M. (in press). Early interventions for children with reading problems: Study designs and preliminary findings. *Learning Disabilities: A Multidisciplinary Journal.*

Greene, J.F. (1993). Systematic phonology: Critical element in teaching reading and language to dyslexics. In S.F. Wright and R. Groner (Eds.), *Facets of dyslexia and its remediation.* Amsterdam: Elsevier Science Publishers.

Greene, J.F. (1996). Psycholinguistic assessment: The critical factors in identifying the dyslexias. *Topics in Language Disorders, 16.*

Greene, J.F. (1996). Effects of an individualized structured language curriculum for middle and high school students. *Annals of Dyslexia, 46.*

Liberman, A.M. (1992). The relation of speech to reading and writing. In R. Frost & L. Katz (Eds.), *Orthography, phonology, morphology, and meaning*. New York: Elsevier Science Publishers.

Moats, L.C. (1997). Directions and research findings: Guide to the California Reading Initiative. *Perspectives, 23*.

Olson, R.K., Wise, B., Ring, J., & Johnson, M. (in press). Computer-based remedial training in phoneme awareness and phonological coding: Effects on the post-training development of word-recognition. *Scientific Studies of Reading*.

Rack, J., Hulme, C., Snowling, M., & Wightman, J. (1994). The role of phonology in young children learning to read words: The direct mapping hypothesis. *Journal of Experimental Child Psychology, 57*.

Robertson, K. (1997). *Phonological awareness and reading achievement in children from differing socio-economic status backgrounds*. Unpublished doctoral dissertation, University of Rhode Island, Kingston.

Samuels, S.J., Schermer, N., & Reinking, D. (1992). Reading fluency: Techniques for making decoding automatic. In S.J. Samuels and A.E. Farstrup (Eds.), *What research has to say about reading instruction* (2nd ed.). Newark, DE: International Reading Association.

Scarborough, H.S., Ehri, L.D., Olson, R.K., & Fowler, A.E. (in press). The fate of phonemic awareness beyond the elementary years. *Scientific Studies of Reading*.

Shankweiler, D., Crain, S., Katz, L., Fowler, A.E., Liberman, A., Brady, S., Thornton, R., Lundquist, E., Dreyer, L., Fletcher, J., Stuebing, K., Shaywitz, S., & Shaywitz, B. (1995). Cognitive profiles of reading-disabled children: Comparison of language skills in phonology, morphology and syntax. *Psychological Science, 6*.

Shankweiler, D., Crain, S., Brady, S., & Macaruso, P. (1992). Identifying the causes of reading disability. In P. B. Gough, L.C. Ehri, & R. Treiman (Eds.), *Reading acquisition*. Hillsdale, NJ: Lawrence Erlbaum Associates.

Torgesen, J.K. (in press). The prevention and remediation of reading disabilities: Evaluating what we know from research. *Academic Language Therapy*.

Vellutino, F.R., Scanlon, D.M., Sipay, E.R., Small, S.G., Pratt, A., Chen, R., & Denckla, M.B. (1997). Cognitive profiles of difficult to remediate and readily remediated poor readers: Early intervention as a vehicle to distinguish between cognitive and experimental deficits as basic causes of specific reading disability. *Journal of Educational Psychology, 88*.

Other Publications of Interest From Sopris West

The *LANGUAGE !* Series

Jane Fell Greene, Ed.D.

A Literacy Intervention Curriculum
Reading, Writing, Spelling, Grammar, Language, Vocabulary
Grades 1-12 and Adults

LANGUAGE ! is the first comprehensive intervention curriculum for students who lack age- or grade-level mastery in reading, writing, and spelling. It fills a void for students in resource, ELL, and inclusion programs. Based on years of literacy research and extensively tested in classrooms, the curriculum's 15 integrated strands are woven sequentially and cumulatively to create a literacy tapestry for at-risk students. Strands include decoding, spelling, comprehension, composition, grammar, vocabulary, mechanics, usage, figurative language, expository and narrative writing, and literature. Practice in reading, writing, and spelling is part of the daily routine throughout the curriculum.

LANGUAGE ! begins by building a broad vocabulary of phonetically regular words, those which constitute 87% of written English. At the same time, phonetically irregular words are introduced and continually retaught for mastery. Vocabulary is expanded by the direct teaching of Anglo-Saxon and Latin roots, prefixes, suffixes, and Greek combining forms, enabling students to access the meanings of some 500,000 English words. Direct teaching of syntax enables students to create and comprehend complex sentences with ease. Students realize independent functioning with high school-level text.

Instructor's Manuals

Jane Fell Greene, Ed.D., Nancy Chapel Eberhardt, M.A., Anne Whitney, Ed.D., CCC-SLP, Louisa Cook Moats, Ed.D.

The Second Edition of *LANGUAGE !* has been designed to integrate **what** to teach with **how** to teach it. The comprehensive *Instructor's Manuals* for Levels 1, 2, and 3 contain information about program objectives, specific instructions for program delivery, and the content and

concepts that students must master to acquire literacy. The *Manuals* also contain answer keys for each of the *Student Mastery Books*, an Introduction written by Louisa C. Moats, and valuable information about the curriculum's philosophical basis.

Instructional Resource Guide for Teachers

Jane Fell Greene, Ed.D., Nancy Chapel Eberhardt, M.A., Anne Whitney, Ed.D., CCC-SLP, Louisa Cook Moats, Ed.D.

The *Instructional Resource Guide for Teachers* contains the resources that teachers need to fully implement the curriculum. The *Guide* takes you from classroom organization, to placement, to teaching the curriculum and contains numerous supports for implementation. The *Guide* also contains a wealth of

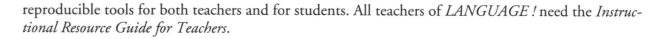

reproducible tools for both teachers and for students. All teachers of *LANGUAGE !* need the *Instructional Resource Guide for Teachers*.

Student Books

The nine *Student Books* (A-I) that correspond directly to the *Instructor's Manual* are not workbooks, but consumable assessment books composed of concept-based tasks that must be mastered. As students master concepts, fluent reading and comprehension skills emerge, as well as written and spoken language skills. Each *Student Book* contains six units. Levels 1, 2, and 3 contain three Student Books each—a total of 9 books with 54 units.

Primary Goals of *LANGUAGE !*

- Comprehensive intervention to provide literacy skills and prepare students for conventional literature instruction

- Individualized, integrated literacy intervention for students with delays in reading, spelling, writing, and language

Main Features

- Research-based

- Affordable

- Comprehensive

- Easy to implement

- Individualized

- Trainer-of-trainers model

- 17 integrated reading/language arts strands

Results

Research shows that middle and high school students gain three years in reading, writing, and spelling ability during an average six-month participation in the curriculum. Elementary students gain about two years during one academic year.

Impact on Instruction

Classroom teachers are trained to deliver the curriculum. No additional staffing is required. Because the curriculum is taught in the classroom by trained teachers, no pullout is needed. On completion of Level 3, students can participate competitively (without accommodation or modification) in general education English and content classes.

Students Served

At-risk, general and special education, Title I, ESL, English language learners, resource, and inclusion students.

Parental Involvement

"Teacher/Parent Pages" and supplementary reading assignments help parents to reinforce the new skills their children are learning.

Training

Because of the *LANGUAGE!* curriculum's linguistic complexity and the importance of proper integration and delivery of its 15 language arts strands, training in the curriculum's content and explicit instructional techniques is strongly recommended for successful implementation. Training is provided as a five-day professional development course for literacy professionals. **For complete information about training, please contact Sopris West at 1-800-547-READ (7323).**

Sounds and Letters Cards

Jane Fell Greene, Ed.D.

Follow *Sounds and Letters* drills with phoneme-grapheme correspondence and word-building activities, using these 166 cards that correspond to the phonemes taught in the *Sounds and Letters* book. Each card bears one phoneme or blend; the cards can be used as flash cards and used with the *Pocket Chart* to build words.

LANGUAGE! Pocket Chart

Students build words and phrases using the *Sounds and Letters Cards* with this *Pocket Chart*. 24 inches wide, with nine rows of clear vinyl pockets and a red backing, the *Chart* can be placed on an easel for easy viewing and access by all students.

Sounds of Our Language Audiotape

This 45-minute audiotape presents phonemes and key words for student practice of letters and blends.

Morphemes for Meaning

Jane Fell Greene, Ed.D.

Expand your students' vocabularies and teach ways of combining morphemes with this set of cards. Mastery of the Anglo-Saxon, Latin, and Greek morphemes (meaningful units of words) helps students access the meanings of more than 500,000 English words. *Morphemes for Meaning* contains suffixes from Anglo-Saxon (Levels 1 and 2); roots, prefixes, and suffixes from Latin (Level 2); and combining forms from Greek (Level 3). Use with the *Pocket Chart*.

LANGUAGE ! Roots

Anne R. Bebko, M.S.T.; John Alexander, M.Ed.; and Richard Doucet, B.A.

This morphologically-based vocabulary supplement contains more than 250 reproducible masters in a sturdy binder. These reproducibles move students from sound-letter correspondence (phonics) to understanding words as units of meaning (morphology), and provide access to the rich vocabulary of the English language. The activities expand student vocabulary by employing roots, prefixes, and suffixes from Latin, and combining forms from Greek. The book is designed to be used with *LANGUAGE !* or on its own, particularly in test preparation programs. *LANGUAGE ! Roots* cultivates comprehension of meanings of English words that are based on Anglo-Saxon, Latin, and Greek morphemes—those words which constitute the vast majority of English.

LANGUAGE ! Categories

Nancy Eberhardt and Denise Powers Sorese

LANGUAGE ! Categories provides practice in important categorization skills, which are the basis for note-taking, formulating a topic sentence, and outlining. Students learn to place groups of words into categories; this provides an intermediate step between learning single words and combining words into sentences and passages. These verbal, written, and kinesthetic exercises are fun for students. The activities are presented as reproducible masters and packaged in a convenient three-ring binder.

LANGUAGE ! Practice

Judy Fell Woods, M.A.

LANGUAGE ! Practice provides teacher-directed activities that support, enrich, and enhance the *LANGUAGE !* curriculum components and offer at-risk elementary learners and English learners the additional practice they need for mastery. The series consists of a *LANGUAGE ! Practice Instructor's Manual* and six consumable workbooks.

J & J Language Readers

Jane Fell Greene, Ed.D., and Judy Fell Woods, M.A.

Research indicates that developing readers require abundant practice in reading decodable, connected text at their independent levels. *J & J Language Readers* provide this practice and more. Each of the 108 stories contains comprehension, language expansion, vocabulary expansion, and higher-level thinking activities. The three-level, 54-unit series exactly matches the *LANGUAGE !* curriculum's scope and sequence. No more searching for reading materials to correspond with the reading/language arts concepts you are teaching! Each level consists of 18 linguistically sequential and cumulative books. The contemporary, multi-ethnic cast includes both older and younger characters, making the series appropriate for many ages.

Sort It!

Sheryl Ferlito, M.A.

Sort It! provides LANGUAGE ! students with word and letter sorting activities that reinforce the vocabulary in Levels 1 and 2. These word sorting activities help facilitate the detection of patterns within words, which, in turn, help improve fluency in reading and spelling. Each activity (36 in all) contains letter sorts (helping students recognize differences between upper and lowercase letters, script and print, etc.), word sorts (rhyming, grammar concepts, spelling, etc.), and concept reviews. These activities encourage students to form generalizations about written words, which help them to eventually link the patterns in new words to known words. The activities are presented as reproducible masters with teacher directions, student tips, and an answer key.

Games and Activities for Readers and Spellers

Debra Coultas, M.A., Anne Whitney, Ed.D.

Enhance phonemic awareness and spelling instruction with simple, engaging multisensory activities that motivate your students. Ideal for intermediate and older learners with reading challenges, *Games and Activities for Readers and Spellers* offers a plethora of games and manipulatives for developing your students' skills in phonemic awareness, syllabication, and spelling. Providing whole class, small group, and individual activities, this program contains:

- More than fifty activities

- Numerous spelling, syllable, and phoneme lists that correspond to the various games

- Suggestions for using it in daily *LANGUAGE !* instruction

- Non-competitive alternatives to learning essential curriculum concepts

Games and Activities for Readers and Spellers includes an 344 page Instructor's Manual containing multisensory activities and reproducibles. The manipulative kit includes a spinner, dice, colored tiles, 30 letter and word cubes, Picture Cards, Word Family Cards, and Letter Cards.

J & J Vocabulary Cards

These boxed sets of vocabulary cards can be used to create sentences, and to practice and check immediate, accurate, fluent word recognition (the number one predictor of comprehension, according to current studies), as well as to pave the road to contextual analysis.

J & J Coloring Book

This coloring book of *J & J* story illustrations is designed especially for elementary students.

J & J Kids Poster

A delightful, colorful poster of the 14 major protagonists in the *J & J* stories.

Degrees of Reading Power® (DRP) BookLink: Literature & Popular Titles

Touchstone Applied Science Associates, Inc.

Using the most scientifically accurate readability assessment, *DRP® Booklink* software provides a list of 12,500 classic literature and leisure titles and their *DRP®* readability levels. *DRP® Booklink* enables you to select appropriate supplementary titles that complement the *LANGUAGE!* curriculum. Choose from among 15 categories, including:

- Adventure
- Mystery
- Classic literature
- Sports
- History
- Science fiction
- Biography

Windows® and Macintosh® compatible CD-ROM or 3.5 diskettes.

For More Information or to Order, Contact

Sopris West

*Helping You Meet the Needs
of At-Risk Students*

**1-800-547-6747
www. sopriswest.com**